746.432

Potter, Cheryl

Ribbon style: knitted
fashions and accessories

W9-BLJ-920

RIBBON Style

CHERYL POTTER

RIBBON Style

Knitted Fashions and Accessories

CREDITS

President ■ Nancy J. Martin

CEO ■ Daniel J. Martin

COO ■ Tom Wierzbicki

Publisher ■ Jane Hamada

Editorial Director ■ Mary V. Green

Managing Editor ■ Tina Cook

Technical Editor ■ Karen Costello Soltys

Copy Editor ■ Durby Peterson

Design Director ■ Stan Green

Illustrator ■ Robin Strobel

Cover and Text Designer ■ Shelly Garrison

Model Photographer ■ John Hamel

Hair and Makeup Stylist ■ Lori Smith

Photography Stylist ■ Pam Simpson

Studio Photographer ■ Brent Kane

Ribbon Style: Knitted Fashions and Accessories
© 2006 by Cheryl Potter

Martingale®
& COMPANY

Martingale & Company
20205 144th Avenue NE
Woodinville, WA 98072-8478 USA
www.martingale-pub.com

No part of this product may be reproduced in any form, unless otherwise stated, in which case reproduction is limited to the use of the purchaser. The written instructions, photographs, designs, projects, and patterns are intended for the personal, noncommercial use of the retail purchaser and are under federal copyright laws; they are not to be reproduced by any electronic, mechanical, or other means, including informational storage or retrieval systems, for commercial use. Permission is granted to photocopy patterns for the personal use of the retail purchaser.

The information in this book is presented in good faith, but no warranty is given nor results guaranteed. Since Martingale & Company has no control over choice of materials or procedures, the company assumes no responsibility for the use of this information.

**Library of Congress
Cataloging-in-Publication Data**

Library of Congress Control Number:
2005033914

ISBN-13: 978-1-56477-668-6

ISBN-10: 1-56477-668-9

Printed in China
11 10 09 08 07 06   8 7 6 5 4 3 2 1

#ANF 8-28-09

and

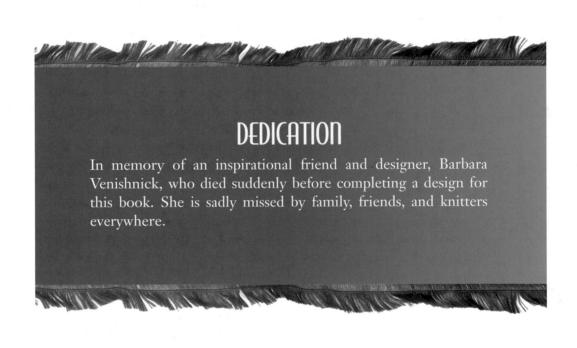

DEDICATION

In memory of an inspirational friend and designer, Barbara Venishnick, who died suddenly before completing a design for this book. She is sadly missed by family, friends, and knitters everywhere.

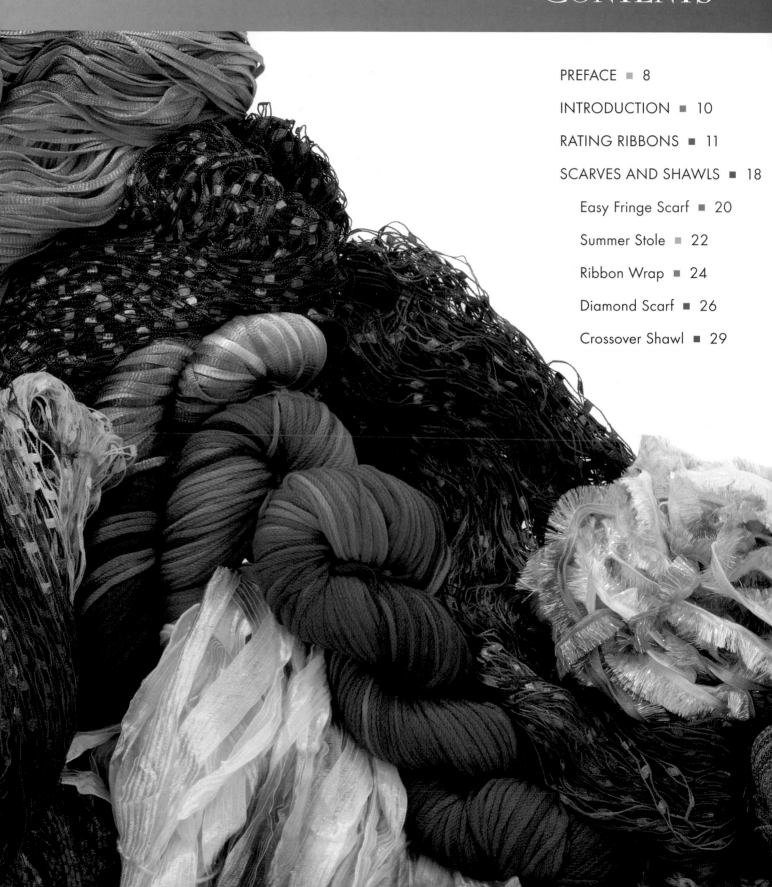

CONTENTS

Preface

While writing my first book, I was introduced to ribbon as yarn by fellow hand painter Patti Subik. Of course, I had seen ribbons and other novelty fibers before and had even tried painting some myself, but truthfully, they scared me. My novice perspective was that ribbon belonged around bouquets at the florist shop or adorning gifts under the Christmas tree. Patti's unique line of fancy ribbons, eyelash yarn, and other novelties opened my eyes.

To my amazement, she categorized anything that could be knit on needles—rickrack, fabric strips, synthetic fur, and even wedding lace—as yarn. I agreed that these trims were outlandishly beautiful—who wouldn't love the look and feel of thick and thin silk fabric fringed with glitter? But, I wondered aloud, who would buy such fanciful edging? Knitters, Patti told me. Knitters with vision, who craved the challenge of achieving a unique designer look. She explained that many knitters had already pushed the envelope with fiber, color, and texture by choosing hand-painted yarns in the first place. Now they were entering

a new realm of knitting by casting on anything they could wind into a ball and reclassify as yarn. Excited by this revelation, I went home and, finding no ribbon, cut up drapery selvage and painted it. It became my first unique novelty yarn, which I called Ribbon Chenille.

Just a few years ago, I couldn't imagine dabbing multicolored dyes across beaded lace or simmering laddered eyelash ribbon in a dye pot. Today, as novelty fibers explode in popularity throughout the yarn market, I think nothing of dousing wide strips of glittered nylon with dye and calling it yarn. Now, caught in the craze of discovering what will be the next wild thing to knit, I hunger for wider and more textured strings and strands that cross over into new categories of yarn. From all the samples I've seen, ribbon entrances me most: wide or narrow, solid or sheer, tubular or flat, shiny or matte.

But one thing still bothered me about ribbon. I wondered if there were numbers of knitters out there that are as tentative about knitting with ribbon as I was when I first began dyeing it. Do they yearn

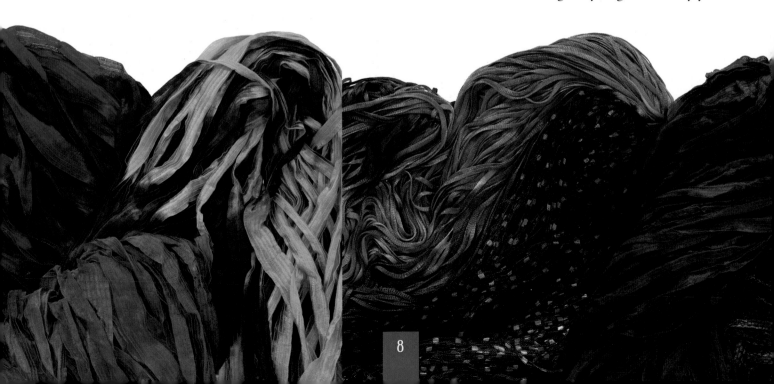

to try slippery nylon mesh but lack the courage to cast on? Judging from the variety of emails and woeful phone calls I receive from accomplished knitters who seek advice about handling ribbon, I believe so. While ribbon yarns are beautiful, they can be quite different to knit than traditional yarns, depending upon fiber construction, needle size used, and preferred stitch pattern. Add to this mix a hand-painted colorway or high-contrast machine print, and you have the recipe for excitement—or disaster.

Sometimes the biggest challenge of knitting with ribbon is winding it into a ball or knitting it before it tangles. I have seen knitters resort to using paper towel rolls, resealable plastic bags, and elastic bands to prevent twisting. And knitters may find that once their yarn is tamed into a ball, they have difficulty locating patterns suited to knitting with ribbon; it's difficult to substitute ribbon in a garment designed for traditional yarns. Patterns for ribbons tend to be yarn-specific, due to the unique nature of ribbon yarn. Ribbons can be difficult to swatch and gauge, because many require huge needles that leave large, lacey holes when knit. On the plus side, knitting with ribbon fits well with the current quick-knit trend—using large needles is a must with most ribbons, and simplicity counts. Many ribbons are so shiny and textured that anything but a bold-yet-easy stitch pattern, such as drop stitch, gets lost.

So why try ribbons at all? Ribbons are difficult to resist: soft to the touch, easy on the eyes, exotic and unique. It is exciting to knit with something that allows any knitter to feel like an instant designer. Ribbons lend distinctive appeal to any garment at a fraction of boutique prices. And as new technology in European mills offers us novel ribbons almost daily, the possibilities for ribbons are endless. Knitters do not have to look for a new animal; it's already here in the form of synthetic strands. Multicomponent ribbons, which are the next generation of what I like to call crossover ribbons, may be the wave of the future.

INTRODUCTION

The inspiration for this book came to me one very trying day at Cherry Tree Hill, my hand-painted yarn company. I was dyeing ribbon yarn for a scarf kit from which all profits would go to the American Cancer Society. One of the ribbons, called Glimmer, was impossible. No matter how careful I was, the yarn fell all over itself. It wound itself around the agitator in the washer, caught on everything in the dryer, and refused to be wound or rolled into a ball. On top of that, knitters were calling weekly to report that the scarves could not be completed because the yarn refused to knit without twisting and tangling. One poor woman who dropped a ball of Glimmer on the floor had resorted to Valium in order to remain calm enough to coax the yarn onto her needles. We tried pairing the ribbon with a fluffy synthetic fur to make it less slippery to knit, we divided it into smaller and more manageable yardage, and still knitters weren't happy.

Rashly, I decided to discontinue Glimmer completely. About a week later, I realized that banishing Glimmer was a short-term solution to a larger problem. More and more ribbon was appearing in the yarn world every day. Since ribbon wasn't going away, knitters needed to know how to knit with it to get the results they expected.

Please use this book as a ribbon reference guide. First, you will find a short introduction to the various types of ribbon currently available on the market, which I have classified into five categories: flat, tubular, ladder, crossover, and multi-component. Next are the projects, grouped into four sections. Each section focuses on particular types of projects, such as "Scarves and Shawls" or "Tanks and Tees." Within each section, the projects use a variety of ribbons and are arranged from simplest to most difficult, with none rated more difficult than intermediate and many designed for the beginning ribbon knitter.

At the start of each project you will find design notes and tips that grew from questions I asked each designer about knitting with ribbon. It is my hope that these insights help you choose ribbon, patterns, and designs for novelty yarns outside the scope of this book. Several of the designs are shown in two ways: knit with hand-painted ribbon and with machine-printed ribbon. This shows you how you can achieve different looks with various ribbons and that substitution in ribbon patterns is possible once you understand the concepts of knitting with ribbon. Don't let the brilliant and highly textured look of these garments intimidate you. Most of the complexity comes from the yarn itself, and once you are comfortable handling ribbon, you will find that the garments are quick to knit and require very little finishing.

Rating RIBBONS

Once I began to explore ribbon yarn I noticed that in addition to being challenging to knit, it was hard to classify. Ribbon can be composed of natural fibers like cotton and silk—I have even hand dyed Merino and Alpaca mesh ribbons—or it can consist of synthetic fibers like nylon and polyester. Sometimes the fibers are combined, such as Merino ribbon with a shiny nylon edge. Ribbons can be cut straight or on the bias. Bias-cut ribbons give a dramatically different diagonal look when knit, due to the drape of the bias-cut mesh fibers. Some are translucent while others are opaque, and ribbon can be finished along the edges or even fringed like eyelash yarn. Another popular ribbon construction is tracked or ladder yarns, which have holes in the center. These fibers run thin to wide and come flat or tubular.

These days there are even crossover ribbons: those that combine more than one basic style. It's possible to find a flat, fringed, bias-cut ribbon in a basket next to a tubular, tracked ribbon in your local yarn shop. For the purpose of this book, I have identified four groups of knitting ribbon and arranged them in order from easiest to hardest to knit: flat, tubular, ladder, and crossover.

Understanding ribbon construction makes handling ribbon easier.

Flat Ribbons

Flat ribbons come as thin as shoelaces and as wide as lasagna noodles—sometimes all within the same ribbon! Wide nylon ribbon tops the popularity chart because it takes dye brilliantly and its width makes it easier to handle than narrow ribbons. Flat ribbons are often shiny, dusted with glitter, or fringed.

One disadvantage to wide ribbons is that they're difficult to unknit and reuse if you make a mistake, because wider ribbon is easily crumpled. Conversely, thinner ribbons are easier to unknit, but harder to rewind into a ball. Some ribbons are so slippery they fall away from themselves, making it difficult to roll them into a ball or keep in a ball while knitting. Shiny equals slippery, especially with thinner flat ribbons, and many knitters resort to containing ribbons that refuse to stick to themselves inside a plastic bag with a resealable closure. This way, the ball can misbehave in the bag without creating something that looks like tangled linguine on your couch.

There are several advantages to knitting with flat ribbons, especially the wider ones. Flat ribbons are easier to knit because they have little texture and contain no loops or holes to catch the needle. Wide ribbons require large-sized needles, and simple stitch patterns show up well. Therefore flat ribbons knit quickly, which means less time knitting and more time wearing the finished garment. Flat ribbon with glitter, variegated color, or fringe gives even the simplest scarf a unique, luxurious, designer look.

Sachet ribbon is 100% nylon and about ¾" wide. You can see how brilliantly it takes color!

Tubular Ribbons

Tubular ribbons have the look of flat ribbon, but are actually constructed as tubes of knit or mesh material that has been flattened. This type of ribbon comes wide or thin, with thin being most popular; thick tubes tend to be heavy on the needle. Tubular ribbons generally have a matte finish, and thus color combinations look duller than those of flat ribbon. Very few tubular ribbons are made of natural fiber, although a few of the projects in this book are made of cotton tubular ribbon. Most tubular ribbons are constructed of machine-made synthetic fibers.

The disadvantages of knitting with tubes are few but important. Because of the double thickness of the flattened tube, the yarn can be cumbersome on the needle and the finished garment warm to wear. The flattened tube can round out if the project is ripped out too many times, so you'll want to keep mistakes or design changes to a minimum. You'll also find it harder to locate patterns for this type of ribbon, simply because so far, it has not been as popular as flat ribbon. The mesh can look plain and often takes hand-dyed color less vibrantly.

On the other hand, tubular ribbon has advantages over other types of ribbon. The biggest advantage is that tubular mesh yarn tends to stick to itself, so winding it into a ball is easy to do, and the yarn stays put. The smooth surface allows for any number of pattern stitches, from simple knit-purl patterns to miters and cables. Another big plus is that the fiber is substantial and great for sturdy items like purses and tote bags.

Pisa is a 100%-nylon tube ribbon that knits into a denser fabric than flat ribbon.

Ladder Ribbons

Ladder ribbons usually have tracks along each edge and openly spaced fiber rungs in between the tracks. They are often called railroad or ladder yarns because the spacing leaves lacy holes in the middle. Lots of times, the tracks on the sides are differently colored and have a different fiber content than ladder rungs. Because they are added later, the additional side wraps that form the tracks are slightly stiffer and stronger than the ladder rungs. This provides the ribbon with more body and better drape than plainer ladders. These yarns range widely, from thin fingering-weight to bulky, and some are highly textured.

Although they're hard to resist in the yarn shop, ladder yarns do have several disadvantages you should be aware of. These openwork ribbons often have substantial spaces between the rungs, and it's easy to catch your needles in these gaps.

Ladder yarn is difficult to wind, tangles easily, and tends to fall off the ball. This kind of ribbon defies gauge, because ladders can be knit on any size needle: large for a loose and open lacey look, or small for a more condensed fabric. They generally require patterns geared specifically for ladder ribbons.

One advantage to choosing ladder ribbon is that although it's relatively expensive, a little goes a long way. Fancy ladders combine texture and color to work well as trim or embellishment for plainer projects. There is nothing better for fringe. Ladder ribbons look complex, and can make the simplest pattern look like a designer original. In this case, the yarn really does the work for you. Some tracked ribbons look like fabric or beaded lace but knit like yarn, producing exciting results.

Windsong is a ladder ribbon with little squares of colorful nylon anchored between two nylon strings or tracks.

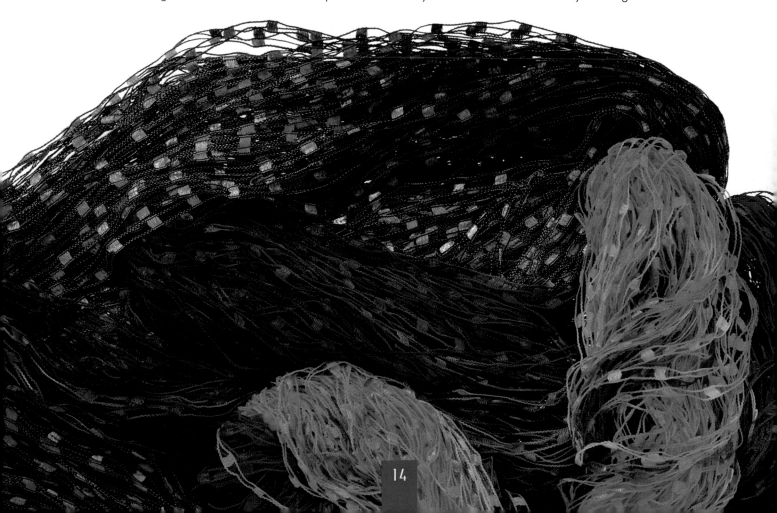

Crossover Ribbons

What I call crossover ribbons are complex yarns exhibiting two or more characteristics of the simpler ribbons discussed previously. They can be any width, and they often are highly textured and contain several different component fibers. In many cases they are multicolored, not only along the length of the ribbon but also across the width. Some of these yarns look more like trims you'd find at a fabric store than what people traditionally think of as ribbon.

A distinct disadvantage of these ribbons is that because of their uniqueness, crossover ribbons have a more limited use than other ribbons. They are also more difficult to find. When you do locate them, knowing what you want to knit and finding the right pattern is essential before buying. Purchasing the right amount of this expensive yarn can also be a problem, because it is difficult to gauge how much to buy when most of these ribbons are sold in low-yardage, 50-gram balls. Once cast on, crossover ribbons can be wider and stiffer than most, refusing to stay on the needle. The complexity of the yarn can be confusing, even when knitting a simple stitch.

With that said, there are also advantages to working with this type of yarn. One big advantage is that simplicity counts—these ribbons often have high-contrast color and texture working together. It is not necessary or advisable to throw a stitch pattern into the mix. Another plus is that complex ribbons are distinct and unique for the discerning ribbon knitter. Crossovers are not as mass-produced as other novelty yarns, and it's easy to create a nouveau garment from fancy ribbon you will find nowhere else. These exciting yarns are the cutting edge of what is new in ribbon, and knitters find it exhilarating to complete an exotic garment from material previously used only as embellishment. Although luxury ribbons can be pricey, you can knit a scarf or shawl for roughly one quarter of what you would pay in an upscale department store or boutique.

Cashcott is wide and flat, but it is constructed as a ladder ribbon.

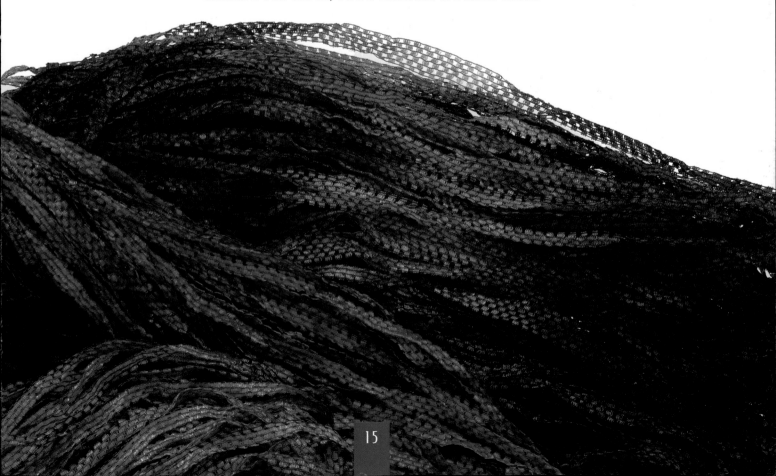

Multicomponent Ribbons

A new wave of ribbon that I call multicomponent yarn is on the horizon. These are trendy novelties that go from one type of ribbon to another—for example, from flat to tubular or to ladder types with fiber or fabric woven through them. Knitters will be pleased to know that the ribbon revolution is still evolving and soon there will be even more interesting things to knit.

Multicomponent ribbons are the newest yarns emerging from European mills.

WINDING RIBBON INTO A BALL

Ribbon is slippery, so I recommend always using a swift to wind it from a hank into a ball. If you don't own a swift, ask the salesclerk where you buy the ribbon to wind it for you on the shop's swift. Below are some pointers for winding a hank of ribbon into a ball.

- If possible, position your swift so that it looks like a Ferris wheel, not a merry-go-round. As you can see in the photograph, this position lets the ribbon flow smoothly without slipping down on itself as you wind it.

- To position the ribbon hank on the swift, first remove the paper label from the hank. Then snap the hank so the ribbon untangles itself and the hank is more or less in a circle.

- Notice that the ribbon hank is tied in a few places. Make sure the ribbon doesn't overlap the ties; if the ribbon strands are flowing in the proper direction, none of them will overlap the ties. Once you have the hank smoothed out, place it on the swift and adjust the circumference of the swift to the size of the hank.

- Make sure that the hank is placed properly on the swift, that is, not twisted. Then open the ties. Often, the beginning and end of the hank are tied together at one spot, and the remaining ties are just short pieces of ribbon or yarn used to hold the ribbon in place. Pull these short pieces out of the hank and discard.

- To wind the ball, take one end of the hank and pull it slightly. If it pulls easily, you can begin winding. If it doesn't pull easily, try the other end of the hank. One end should be on top and one end underneath all the strands of ribbon. To make the winding progress more smoothly, spread the ribbon out evenly on the surface of the swift rather than having it all clumped together in the center.

- If you run into difficulty using a ball winder in conjunction with the swift, you can simply take the ribbon off of the ball winder and wind it by hand. But leave the hank on the swift to prevent tangles as you go. Merely wind from the swift by hand instead of using the mechanical ball winder.

- Keep the ribbon taut as you wind it so that the ball will not disintegrate as it is being formed.

- If you find a tangle, note that this generally happens only at the beginning and end of the hank, and it's the result of overlapping strands. You may need to pass the ball of ribbon through a few loops of ribbon on the swift to untangle it. Rather than taking the ribbon off the swift, simply wind the ribbon by hand for a few revolutions, and then put it on the ball winder to continue.

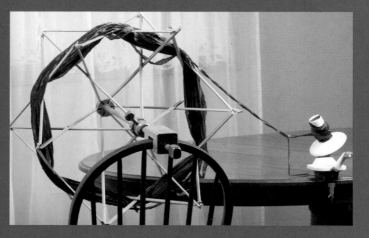

SCARVES AND SHAWLS

Knitting with ribbon can be daunting, because ribbon can appear much different in a ball or hank than it does when knit in a garment. It is often impossible to visualize how it will look when knit until you complete a swatch. Therefore, starting with scarves and shawls is a natural choice for beginning ribbon knitters: these projects require little to no shaping, allowing the knitter to focus strictly on the process of knitting with new and different fibers. Scarves, especially, require no sizing, and other considerations such as gauge can become secondary as knitters get comfortable with the feel of knitting with ribbon.

EASY FRINGE SCARF

By JoAnne Turcotte

This scarf is a perfect first ribbon project because the easy knitting allows beginning ribbon knitters to get comfortable handling this type of yarn. The only challenge is the fringe, which is created by dropping stitches and letting them open and unravel—a concept JoAnne first noticed in a recent book by Nicki Epstein. This finish work encourages the knitter to develop confidence and control when working with ribbon, which will carry over into more challenging projects.

As their names suggest, the only difference between Fringe and Glitter Fringe ribbons is the glitter, so they can be easily substituted for one another. Not nearly as slippery as some ribbons, they can be wound by hand into a ball that won't self-destruct, as happens with many ribbons. Both Fringe and Glitter Fringe are elaborate ribbons that need only a simple stitch to show them off. The simple eyelet stitch prevents the edges of the scarf from rolling, plus it's open and airy, which makes the side stitches easy to unravel. Unraveling stitches with a ribbon can be a slippery process. Sit at a table with the scarf flat in front of you for maximum control.

The glitter and shine of Fringe, shown in Champlain Sunset, gives this simple project glamour. For a dressier look, substitute Glitter Fringe as seen on the next page.

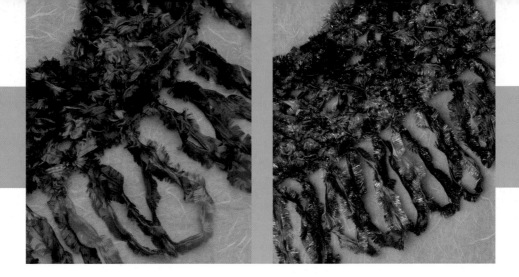

Vital Statistics

Skill Level: Beginner

Size: 5" x 65" (6" x 55")

Gauge: Approx 2 sts = 1"

Ribbon Type: Bulky-weight flat with fringe edges

Materials

Yarn is from Cherry Tree Hill.

Yarn: 1 hank of Fringe or Glitter Fringe (100% nylon; 4 oz; 62 yds) in colorway Champlain Sunset (Fringe) or Green Mountain Madness (Glitter Fringe)

Needles: US 19

Notions: Stitch marker

Fringe, an eyelash ribbon, is shown in Champlain Sunset (top), and Glitter Fringe is shown in Green Mountain Madness (bottom).

Scarf Instructions

Loosely CO 10 (12) sts.

Row 1: P1, (YO, P2tog) 3 (4) times, PM, K3.

Row 2: K3, SM, P1, *(YO, P2tog); rep from * to end of row.

Row 3: P1, (YO, P2tog) 3 (4) times, SM, K3.

Repeat rows 2 and 3 until almost out of yarn, ending with row 3.

On the next RS row, K3, remove marker, BO rem sts pw.

Drop the 3 rem sts off the needle and unravel them with your fingers. Tie each dropped-st loop into an overhand knot. Shake and pull to anchor in place.

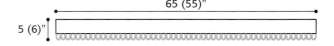

65 (55)"

5 (6)"

KNIT WITH SUCCESS

Although Fringe and Glitter Fringe yarns knit easily, knitters too often become concerned with keeping the ribbon straight and flat as they knit. Actually, there is little difference between knitting when the ribbon is flat or when it's allowed to softly twist. If you're experiencing extreme twisting, lock the ball in a resealable plastic bag and let it dangle as you hold the exiting strand in the air; the weight of the ball will cause the yarn to slowly untwist.

SUMMER STOLE

By JoAnne Turcotte

A photo from the 1940s inspired this easy-to-knit stole. In the photo, designer JoAnne Turcotte's mother is pictured wearing a fox stole that wraps around both shoulders and latches in the front. JoAnne updated the look with a wide flat ribbon called Sachet.

The stole is worked in the round, and the fabric is gathered in the front with a knitted band that simulates the front latch. A simple eyelet pattern stitch locks the ribbon into place and minimizes the movement of the stitches while showing off the sleekness of the ribbon. The ribbon is so light and lofty that even a wide stole like this can be easily gathered in a small area without creating lots of bulk. The shine of Sachet lends this project a level of elegance, producing a lightweight garment that works up quickly on large needles.

This stole softly covers the shoulders and requires only one hank of Sachet.
The model is shown in colorway Martha's Vineyard.

Finish the stole with a single wrapped band.

Vital Statistics

Skill Level: Beginner

Size: 12" x 32" (10" x 37")

Gauge: 8 sts = 4" in patt

Ribbon Type: Wide flat

Materials

Yarn is from Cherry Tree Hill.

Yarn: 1 hank of Sachet (100% nylon; 4 oz; 121 yds) in colorway Martha's Vineyard

Needles: US 17 and US 11

Sachet in colorway Martha's Vineyard

Stole Instructions

Using larger needles, loosely CO 63 (73) sts. Join, taking care not to twist sts.

Rnd 1: Knit.

Rnd 2: K1, *(YO, K2tog); repeat from * around.

Rep rnds 1 and 2 until almost out of yarn, ending with knit rnd, and leaving about 1 yd of ribbon for wrap.

BO all sts.

Finishing

Weave in all ends.

Using smaller needles and rem ribbon, CO 7 sts. Work in St st for 4½". BO all sts. Gather center front of stole and wrap knitted band around front gathered section. Sew CO edge to BO edge of band and anchor on inside of stole.

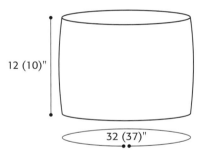

12 (10)"

32 (37)"

KNIT WITH SUCCESS

Sachet is a true ribbon, complete with the inherent slipperiness. It likes to flow, so to tame this wild spirit, wind the Sachet into a soft ball by hand, place the yarn in a resealable bag, and seal it shut. When knitting, pull out a few yards of ribbon and reseal the bag. The yarn will twist and tangle less when it's contained this way, and your knitting will progress like a breeze.

Ribbon WRAP

By Carla Esden-Tempska

When designer Carla first saw the Glitter Sachet ribbon, she was so impressed with the lovely sheen and hand-painted color-way that she simply wished to wrap herself up in it, and the Ribbon Wrap was born. A simple, loose garter stitch was all it took to transform the ribbon into a stable fabric that shows off the glitter. This easy-to-wear wrap is a wonderful accessory to dress up any outfit. It has a luxurious and dramatic look highlighted by a dusting of glitter. For a subtler look, try substituting Sachet for Glitter Sachet.

Be aware that garments knit from ribbon yarn tend to stretch with wear, especially shawls and scarves. And the looser the stitches, the more the knit fabric stretches, making gauging a loosely knit ribbon project difficult. The gauge for this wrap after it has been stretched with wear is about five stitches to four inches, so use this information in determining how many stitches to add if you wish to make your shawl longer than the one shown. Loose knitters should try size 17 needles while tight knitters may need size 19 needles to achieve gauge.

The Ribbon Wrap is shown in Glitter Sachet in colorway Spring Frost.

The Ribbon Wrap shown in an alternate yarn, Sachet,
in colorway Indian Summer, lends the wrap
a warmer, less glitzy look.

Vital Statistics

Skill Level: Beginner

Size: 14" x 66" after blocking, excluding fringe

Gauge: 5 sts = 4" when stretched

Ribbon Type: Wide flat

Materials

Yarn is from Cherry Tree Hill.

Yarn: 2 hanks of Glitter Sachet (99% nylon/1% metallic polyester; 4 oz; 131 yds) in colorway Spring Frost

Needles: US 17 straight needles; US 17 circular needle, 29" long

Notions: Size J (6 mm) crochet hook

Glitter Sachet in colorway Spring Frost

Wrap Instructions

Cut 68 pieces, 22" long, for fringe and set aside.

CO 82 sts.

Work 64 rows in garter st. BO all sts loosely.

Finishing

Block finished rectangle to 14" x 66". Spray lightly with water. Stretch wrap and pin to dimensions until dry.

Using crochet hook or your fingers, attach 2 pieces of fringe at each corner and at every 2nd garter ridge at short ends of shawl (see "Fringe" on page 104).

66" (excluding fringe)

14"

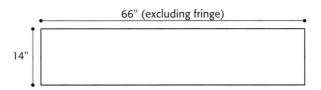

KNIT WITH SUCCESS

Because Glitter Sachet can be a bit slippery, Carla recommends working with wooden or bamboo needles. She also recommends fringing ribbon shawls—the longer the fringe, the better. Unlike many yarns, this wide flat ribbon does not tangle easily, and you don't need many strands to create fringe with great drape and body.

DIAMOND SCARF

By Donna Druchunas

Designer Donna Druchunas wanted to capitalize on the popularity of scarves while avoiding the ubiquitous triangle or long rectangle. Her challenge was to use a crossover ribbon to create an easy-to-knit project with a completely different look. The simple garter-stitch mitered squares are easy enough for confident beginners, and experienced knitters will have fun watching the edges undulate as each diamond shape appears.

This funky design is equally suited for casual or dressy wear. The sheen of the yarn makes this scarf perfect for an evening out, and the unusual shape makes it a fun accent for jeans and a tank top for a weekend on the town. The lightweight sparkly ribbon creates a shimmering scarf that is comfortable for year-round wear.

This knitted jewelry, like other classic pieces, will become a staple in your wardrobe.

This nontraditional scarf is shown in Cashcott ribbon in colorway Tropical Storm.

Vital Statistics

Skill Level: Easy

Size: Approx 5½" x 56" (width is measured at widest point)

Gauge: Approx 2½ sts = 1" in garter st

Ribbon Type: Crossover (wide flat, ladder)

Materials

Yarn is from Cherry Tree Hill.

Yarn: 1 hank of Cashcott (100%-nylon novelty ribbon; 4 oz; 140 yds) in colorway Tropical Storm

Needles: US 15

Caschcott in colorway Tropical Storm

Garter Stitch

Knit all rows.

Diamond Pattern

Setup Row: K11, sl 2, K1, p2sso, K11.

Row 1: K11, P1, K11.

Row 2: K10, sl 2, K1, p2sso, K10.

Row 3: K10, P1, K10.

Row 4: K9, sl 2, K1, p2sso, K9.

Row 5: K9, P1, K9.

Row 6: K8, sl 2, K1, p2sso, K8.

Row 7: K8, P1, K8.

Row 8: K7, sl 2, K1, p2sso, K7.

Row 9: K7, P1, K7.

Row 10: K6, sl 2, K1, p2sso, K6.

Row 11: K6, P1, K6.

Row 12: K5, sl 2, K1, p2sso, K5.

Row 13: K5, P1, K5.

Row 14: K4, sl 2, K1, p2sso, K4.

Row 15: CO 8 sts at beg of row, K12, P1, K4 (see "Cable Cast On" on page 102).

Row 16: CO 8 sts at beg of row, K11, sl 2, K1, p2sso, K11.

KNIT WITH SUCCESS

Cashcott is a wide, loosely woven ribbon. As you're knitting, take care not to pierce the yarn with the needle points. Because this project is knit on size 15 needles, they can leave a big hole in the ribbon if you do pierce it. To correct this situation if it happens, pull the fibers back into position by gently tugging on the section of ribbon that was pierced.

Scarf Instructions

Loosely CO 25 sts.

Work setup row of diamond pattern once.

Work rows 1–16 of diamond pattern 9 times.

Work rows 1–14 once more.

Work ending point as foll:

    Row 1: K4, P1, K4.

    Row 2: K3, sl 2, K1, p2sso, K3.

Row 3: K3, P1, K3.

Row 4: K2, sl 2, K1, p2sso, K2.

Row 5: K2, P1, K2.

Row 6: K1, sl 2, K1, p2sso, K1.

Row 7: K1, P1, K1.

Row 8: Sl 2, K1, p2sso; 1 st rem.

Fasten off and weave in all ends.

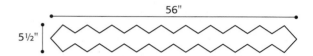

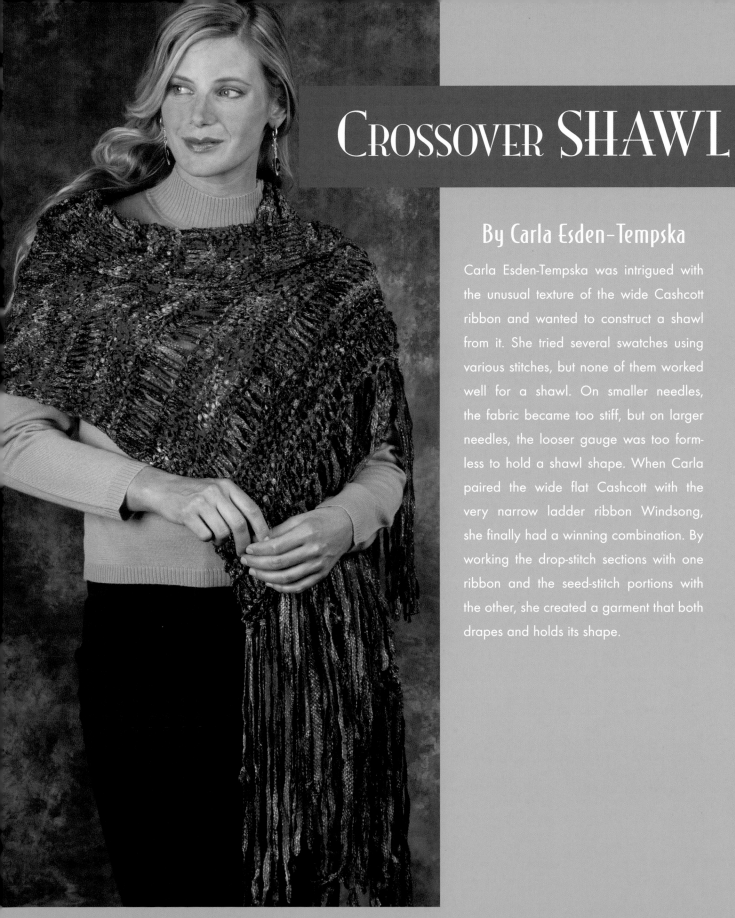

Crossover SHAWL

By Carla Esden-Tempska

Carla Esden-Tempska was intrigued with the unusual texture of the wide Cashcott ribbon and wanted to construct a shawl from it. She tried several swatches using various stitches, but none of them worked well for a shawl. On smaller needles, the fabric became too stiff, but on larger needles, the looser gauge was too formless to hold a shawl shape. When Carla paired the wide flat Cashcott with the very narrow ladder ribbon Windsong, she finally had a winning combination. By working the drop-stitch sections with one ribbon and the seed-stitch portions with the other, she created a garment that both drapes and holds its shape.

This versatile shawl is knit from two ladder ribbons, Cashcott and Windsong, stranded together. Both ribbons are in colorway River Run.

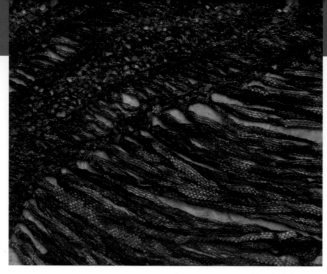

This shimmering shawl appears redesigned as a poncho on page 89.

Vital Statistics

Skill Level: Easy

Size: 22" x 54", excluding fringe

Gauge: 7 sts = 4" in patt

Ribbon Types: Cashcott—crossover (wide flat, ladder); Windsong (narrow ladder)

Materials

Yarns are from Cherry Tree Hill.

Yarn:

A—3 hanks of Cashcott (100% nylon; 4 oz; 140 yds) in colorway River Run

B—2 hanks of Windsong (100% nylon; 50 g; 165 yds) in colorway River Run

Needles: US 15

Notions: Size J (6 mm) crochet hook

Cashcott (top) and Windsong (bottom),
both in colorway River Run

Stitch Patterns

Seed Stitch

Row 1: *K1, P1, rep from * to end.

Row 2: *P1, K1, rep from * to end.

Twisted Drop Stitch

Put right-hand needle through next st on left needle as if to knit. Wrap yarn around both needles once. Then wrap yarn around right-hand needle only and complete st by pulling right-needle wrap through both loops on left needle.

KNIT WITH SUCCESS

Carla chose seed stitch because she liked the way it blends colors of hand-dyed yarns rather than creates shade lines. She added occasional rows of twisted drop stitch to emphasize the wide Cashcott ribbon. Alternating two seed-stitch rows of Cashcott with two rows of Windsong married the two yarns to create a durable fabric with both texture and drape. They blended so well that it is difficult to tell that the garment is knit from two widely different yarns.

Shawl Instructions

From A, cut 108 pieces, 28" long, for fringe and set aside.

Using A, CO 50 sts.

Knit 3 rows.

Beg patt row sequence as foll:

Using 2 strands of B, work 2 rows seed st.

Using 1 strand of A, work 2 rows seed st.

Using 2 strands of B, work 2 rows seed st.

Using 1 strand of A, work 1 row seed st.

Cont with 1 strand of A, knit 1 row.

Work twisted drop st row: K1, work 48 twisted drop sts, K1.

Knit 2 rows.

Repeat this sequence of rows until shawl is approx 70" long or desired length.

Knit 1 row with A.

BO all sts loosely.

Using 2 strands of A held tog, attach fringe at evenly spaced intervals along short ends of shawl (see "Fringe" on page 104).

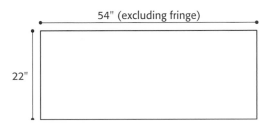

54" (excluding fringe)

22"

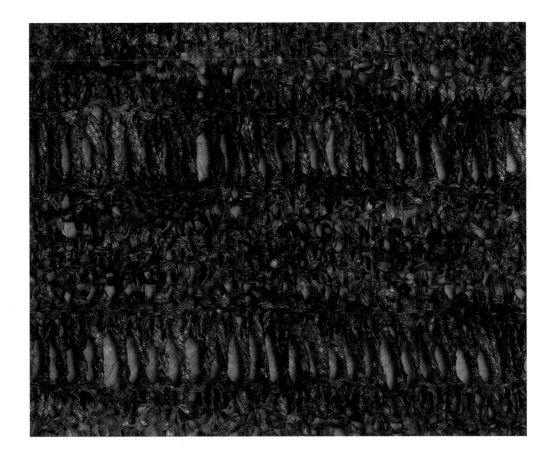

SHIMMER SHAWL

By Cheryl Potter

Years ago I designed a triangular shawl using Jumbo Loop, a large-loop mohair bouclé. I wanted to knit the same shape using Sachet ribbon but was concerned that the heaviness of the ribbon might cause the shawl to stretch out of shape. My solution was to combine the Sachet with the original Jumbo Loop mohair. While this mohair looks heavy, it is actually light and bouncy. Knit in garter stitch, it creates stability and visual interest in the shawl and prevents stretching. In contrast, the Sachet portions are knit in stockinette stitch to emphasize the ribbon's shine.

An alternate version of this shawl knit in a lighter-weight mohair and a narrower ribbon is shown on page 35. That shawl is knit using the same pattern stitch, but it has a completely different gauge.

This basic version of the Shimmer Shawl is knit in alternating sections of Jumbo Loop and Glitter Sachet. Both yarns are shown in colorway Monet.

The Shimmer Shawl doubles as a cozy throw.

Vital Statistics

Skill Level: Easy

Size: Approx 50" x 31", excluding fringe

Gauge: 2½ sts = 1"

Ribbon Type: Wide flat

Materials

Yarns are from Cherry Tree Hill.

Yarn:

A—1 hank Jumbo Loop Mohair (99% mohair/1% nylon binder; 8 oz; 185 yds) in colorway Monet

B—2 hanks Glitter Sachet (99% nylon/1% metallic polyester; 4 oz; 131 yds) in colorway Monet

Needle: US 13 circular needle, 29" long

Notions: 4.5 mm crochet hook

Jumbo Loop Mohair (top) and Glitter Sachet (bottom), both in colorway Monet

Shawl Instructions

With A, CO 3 sts.

Row 1: Knit.

Row 2: Knit, inc 1 st at beg and end of row: 5 sts.

Row 3: Knit.

Row 4: Change to B, but do not cut A. Knit, inc 1 st at beg and end of row: 7 sts.

Row 5: Purl.

Row 6: Change to A, and knit, inc 1 st at beg and end of row: 9 sts.

Repeat rows 1–6, switching between 2 yarns as indicated and carrying unused yarn along edge until there are 115 sts or you've reached your desired length.

BO loosely and weave in ends.

KNIT WITH SUCCESS

Yarns are alternated on even-numbered rows. Don't cut the yarns when they're not in use. Instead, carry them loosely up the side of the garment to prevent puckering. When you fringe the shawl, the carried yarn won't be noticeable.

Finishing

Block lightly by setting iron to "steam" and moving it over garment without touching. Pin damp fabric to dimensions and let dry.

Cut remaining yarn B into 15" lengths for fringe. Attach 3 strands at a time to EOR by folding in half and looping through row ends with crochet hook. Pull taut to secure (see "Fringe" on page 104).

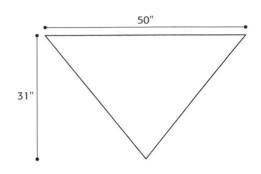

FROTH SHIMMER SHAWL

By Cheryl Potter

This lightweight version of the Shimmer Shawl on page 32 is perfect for cool evenings. It's the same triangle shape, and it uses the same types of yarn: mohair and a flat ribbon. The main difference is that the two yarns in this project are both lighter-weight than those used in the basic Shimmer Shawl. Making a shawl of about the same size requires merely knitting more rows in the same pattern.

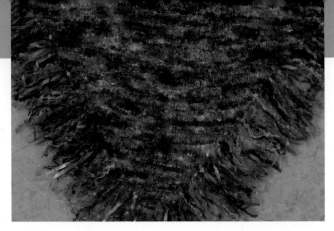

Changing the yarn size and colorway gives this version of
the Shimmer Shawl a more delicate look.

Vital Statistics

Skill Level: Easy

Size: Approx 42" x 29", excluding fringe

Gauge: 3½ sts = 1"

Ribbon Type: Narrow flat

Materials

Yarns are from Cherry Tree Hill.

Yarn:

A—1 hank Froth Mohair Bouclé (99% mohair/1% nylon binder; 8 oz; 650 yds) in colorway Silver Streak

B—1 hank Baby Sachet (100% nylon; 4 oz; 345 yds) in colorway Silver Streak

Needle: US 10 circular needle, 29" long

Notions: 4.5 mm crochet hook

Froth Mohair Bouclé (top) and Baby Sachet (bottom),
both in colorway Silver Streak

Shawl Instructions

With A, CO 3 sts.

Row 1: Knit.

Row 2: Knit, inc 1 st at beg and end of row: 5 sts.

Row 3: Knit.

Row 4: Change to B, but do not cut A. Knit, inc 1 st at beg and end of row: 7 sts.

Row 5: Purl.

Row 6: Change to A, and knit, inc 1 st at beg and end of row: 9 sts.

Rep rows 1–6, switching between 2 yarns as indicated and carrying unused yarn up the side until there are 171 sts or you've reached your desired length.

BO loosely and weave in ends.

Finishing

Block lightly by setting iron to "steam" and moving it over garment without touching. Pin damp fabric to dimensions and let dry.

Cut remaining A and B into 14" lengths for fringe. Attach 2 strands of A and 1 strand of B at a time to EOR by folding strands in half and looping them through row ends with crochet hook (see "Fringe" on page 104).

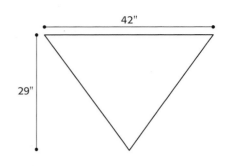

TANKS AND TEES

Ribbon is an obvious choice for knitting short-sleeved or sleeveless tops because it transforms these wardrobe staples into versatile pieces of wearable art. They can be worn year-round in any climate and can slip easily under a suit coat or look just as fabulous topping a favorite pair of jeans. Ribbons know no age barrier—these trendy tanks and tees will attract teens and moms alike. While ribbons can be expensive, these lightweight garments do not require much yarn, and they add pizzazz to any outfit for surprisingly little money compared to the cost of knitting a jacket or cardigan. Most of all, these simple garments are as fun to knit as they are to wear. These quick-knit projects will seem to fly from your needles.

PISA TANK

By Jill Ramos

Designer Jill Ramos's timeless, all-season garment can be dressed up or down and would look just as nice with summer shorts as under a suit jacket or blazer in the fall. The overall simplicity of this project focuses attention on the multicolored ribbon, allowing it to shine. The tank is knit in simple stockinette with minimal edging around the armhole and neck, a perfect beginner project.

Using ribbon in a simple tank allows knitters to achieve a luxury look. An easy yarn like Pisa encourages any knitter to create this versatile garment with minimal effort. Because the tank is knit on smaller needles to give the ribbon a firmer hand, it's easy to measure gauge and therefore also possible to substitute other yarns and ribbons. For a more casual wash-and-wear garment, all-cotton Rainbow Ribbon is a great choice.

Pisa Tank is knit in Pisa, a nylon tubular ribbon, in colorway Silver Streak. It goes effortlessly from a day at the beach to the boardroom.

Vital Statistics

Skill Level: Intermediate

Finished Bust Measurement: 35 (37, 39, 41)"

Length: 19 (20, 21, 22)"

Gauge: 20 sts and 26 rows = 4" in St st

Ribbon Type: Tubular

Materials

Yarn is from Cherry Tree Hill.

Yarn: 3 (3, 4, 4) hanks of Pisa (100% nylon; 4 oz; 248 yds) in colorway Silver Streak

Needles: US 7 straight needles; US 7 circular needle, 16" long, or size needed to obtain gauge

Notions: Stitch holders

Pisa in colorway Silver Streak

Back

With straight needles, CO 87 (93, 97, 103) sts. Work in St st until piece measures 11½ (12½, 13, 14)" from beg. End with a WS row.

Armhole shaping: BO 2 sts at beg of each row 12 times (24 sts total dec), then dec 1 st each side every foll 4th row 0 (1, 2, 3) times: 63 (67, 69, 73) sts rem. Cont in patt until piece measures 18 (19, 20, 21)" from beg. End with a WS row.

Back neck shaping: Work 18 (20, 20, 22) sts. Slip next 27 (27, 29, 29) sts to holder. Attach a 2nd ball and work rem 18 (20, 20, 22) sts. Working both sides at once, BO 3 sts at each neck edge twice, then BO 2 sts at each neck edge once: 10 (12, 12, 14) sts rem.

Work even until piece measures 19 (20, 21, 22)".

Slip rem sts to holder.

Front

Work as for back until piece measures 14 (14½, 15, 16)" from beg. End with a WS row.

Front neck shaping: Cont working armhole decs, and AT THE SAME TIME, work to center 27 (27, 29, 29) sts and sl them to holder. Attach 2nd ball and work to end of row. Work 1 row even on each side. Dec 1 st at neck edge every 4th row 8 times.

Work even on rem 10 (12, 12, 14) sts on each shoulder until piece measures same as back.

Sl rem sts to holder.

Finishing

Hand wash pieces in cool water. Block to finished measurements and lay flat to dry.

Join front to back at shoulders using 3-needle BO (see page 105).

Sew side seams.

Armholes: With RS facing, use 16" circular needle to PU 78 (78, 82, 82) sts. BO pw on next row.

KNIT WITH SUCCESS

Pisa is a shiny nylon ribbon that tends to stick to itself better than do most other nylon ribbons. Even so, Jill recommends winding Pisa on a swift, if possible, and storing the balls in resealable bags when not in use. Otherwise, treat Pisa like any other yarn. Knitters who allow it to twist naturally without trying to straighten the ribbon stitch by stitch will be pleased by the bits of random textural interest Pisa offers.

Your garment will be enhanced by the texture Pisa produces if you let the ribbon "do its own thing."

Neck: Using circular needle, beg at back with RS facing, knit all sts on back holder. *PU 2 sts, skip 1 st, rep from * around to front holder. Work all sts on front holder. *PU 2 sts, skip 1 st, rep from * to back sts. BO pw on next row.

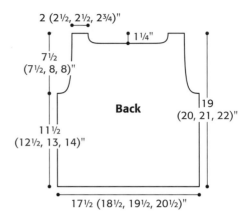

2 (2½, 2½, 2¾)"

1¼"

7½
(7½, 8, 8)"

Back

19
(20, 21, 22)"

11½
(12½, 13, 14)"

17½ (18½, 19½, 20½)"

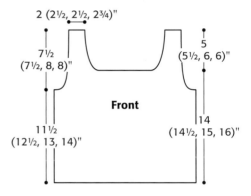

2 (2½, 2½, 2¾)"

7½
(7½, 8, 8)"

5
(5½, 6, 6)"

Front

11½
(12½, 13, 14)"

14
(14½, 15, 16)"

Eros Extreme Short-Sleeved Top

By JoAnne Turcotte

JoAnne Turcotte enjoys designing for beginning knitters. In this easy-to-knit garment she used simple reverse stockinette stitch because the ribbon's texture and variegated color produce an exciting fabric by themselves, allowing her to create an alluring sweater with minimal effort. The ribbon enhances a basic garment, creating shimmer and shine and adding a texture that feels like knitted beads.

This simple, short-sleeved sweater is perfect for the knitter who wants a glamorous garment but doesn't want a sleeveless top. It offers more coverage but without a matronly look. This design fills the need for style and adds pizzazz because either ribbon choice—Eros Extreme or Cashcott—allows for a draping effect and also has enough elasticity to create a body-hugging shape.

The Eros Extreme tee is knit in Eros Extreme from Plymouth Yarn Company.

For a hand-painted look, try the same design in Cherry Tree Hill's Cashcott, shown here in Indian Summer.

Vital Statistics

Skill Level: Beginner

Finished Bust Measurement: 36 (40, 44, 48)"

Length: 20 (20, 21, 21)"

Gauge: 10 sts = 4" on US 15 needles in rev St st

Ribbon Type: Crossover (wide flat, ladder)

Materials

Yarn is from Cherry Tree Hill unless otherwise noted.

Yarn: 5 (6, 6, 7) balls of Eros Extreme from Plymouth Yarn Company (100% nylon; 100 g; 98 yds) in color 114

or 4 (5, 5, 5) hanks of Cashcott (100% nylon; 4 oz; 143 yds) in Indian Summer

Needles: US 13 and 15 straight needles; US 13 circular needle, 16" long, or size needed to obtain gauge

Notions: Stitch markers, size J (6 mm) crochet hook (optional)

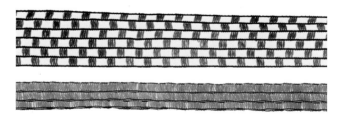

Eros Extreme, color 114 (top), and Cashcott, Indian Summer (bottom)

K1, P1 Ribbing

Row 1 (RS): P1, *(K1, P1); rep from * to end.

Row 2: K1, *(P1, K1); rep from * to end.

Rep rows 1 and 2 for rib patt.

Reverse Stockinette Stitch

All RS rows: Purl.

All WS rows: Knit.

Back and Front (Make 2)

With smaller needles, loosely CO 43 (47, 53, 57) sts for the back. Work in K1, P1 ribbing for 1", ending with a WS row, and inc 2 (3, 2, 3) sts evenly across last row of ribbing: 45 (50, 55, 60) sts.

Change to larger needles and begin working in rev St st until total length measures 18 (18, 19, 19)", ending with WS (knit) row.

Shape neck: Work across 14 (16, 18, 20) sts. Turn, work back. Dec 1 st at neck edge (K2tog) of next 3 WS rows: 11 (13, 15, 17) sts. Work even until total length is 20 (20, 21, 21)", ending with WS row. BO shoulder sts. Reattach yarn to neck edge and BO next 17 (18, 19, 20) sts. Work to end: 14 (16, 18, 20) sts. Work 1 row even. Dec 1 st (ssk) at neck edge of next 3 RS rows: 11 (13, 15, 17) sts. Work even until total length is 20 (20, 21, 21)", ending with WS row. BO all sts.

Sleeves (Make 2)

With smaller needles, loosely CO 33 (33, 35, 35) sts. Work in K1, P1 ribbing for 1", ending with WS row and inc 2 sts on last row of ribbing: 35 (35, 37, 37) sts.

Change to larger needles, and work in rev St st, inc 1 st at each side edge on the 3rd and every foll 4th row until there are 41 (41, 43, 43) sts.

Work even until total length is 5", ending with WS row. BO loosely.

KNIT WITH SUCCESS

When knitting scarves first became quite popular, a ribbon yarn called Eros arrived on the scene. It was pretty and colorful, but it had wide, open tracks that were easy to catch on knitting needles. Eros Extreme and Cashcott are wider ribbons made with smaller tracks and are therefore easier to knit. So if you've ever tried Eros and been discouraged, you'll be pleasantly surprised by this second generation of that yarn.

Both Eros Extreme and Cashcott come in hank form and are easy to wind into a ball by hand without any fuss. Eros Extreme comes in a small-circumference hank that can be wound while holding the yarn around one arm. Because these ribbons aren't slippery, they're easy to handle and knit, making them great choices for a first ribbon project.

Finishing

Sew shoulder seams.

With sweater laid out flat, wrong sides on table, measure 8¼ (8¼, 8½, 8½)" from shoulder seams and place st marker at this position on fronts and backs. Pin sleeves in place between these markers and then sew in sleeves.

Sew side and underarm seams using rem ribbon.

Neck edging: Using circular needle, PU 52 (54, 56, 58) sts around neck edge. Join, and purl 1 rnd. BO kw.

Alternate neck edging: Work 1 rnd crab st (rev sc) around neck edge with size J crochet hook (see "Reverse Single Crochet" on page 103).

Weave in all ends.

No blocking is needed.

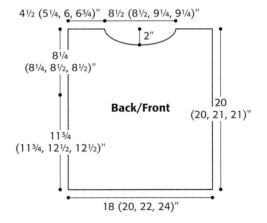

4½ (5¼, 6, 6¾)"   8½ (8½, 9¼, 9¼)"   2"

8¼ (8¼, 8½, 8½)"

11¾ (11¾, 12½, 12½)"

Back/Front

20 (20, 21, 21)"

18 (20, 22, 24)"

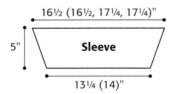

16½ (16½, 17¼, 17¼)"

5"

Sleeve

13¼ (14)"

ALL THAT JAZZ

By Donna Druchunas

The simple shaping of this traditional T-shirt top really shows off the shimmering texture of the yarn. To pique interest, designer Donna Druchunas used an easy-to-knit combination of stockinette and garter stitch stripes. The addition of a scalloped bottom edge gives a feminine touch. If worked in regular cotton yarn, this basic tee might be boring, but ribbon transforms it into a striking garment that can be worn to the office or an evening party.

The knit fabric that Pisa ribbon creates provides cool comfort next to your skin without the open weave of many summer sweaters—there's no need for a camisole or tank under this warm-weather sweater.

All That Jazz is a cool summer tee that provides full coverage. The tee is shown in Pisa ribbon in colorway Serengeti.

Vital Statistics

Skill Level: Intermediate

Finished Bust Measurement: 38 (41½, 45½, 49)"

Gauge: 20 sts = 4" in St st

Ribbon Type: Tubular

Materials

Yarn is from Cherry Tree Hill.

Yarn: 5 hanks Pisa (100% nylon; 4 oz; 248 yds) in colorway Serengeti

Needles: US 8 or size needed to obtain gauge; US 8 circular needle, 16" long

Pisa in colorway Serengeti

Pattern Stitch

This pattern combines 8 rows of St st with 6 rows of garter st to make a textured stripe.

Row 1 (RS): Knit.

Row 2: Purl.

Rows 3–8: Repeat rows 1 and 2.

Rows 9–14: Knit.

Repeat rows 1–14 for patt.

Back and Front (Make 2)

Scalloped edging: CO 5 sts. K1, M1, knit to end. Turn and rep this row until you have 10 (11, 12, 13) sts; 1 scallop made. Cut yarn, leaving tail to weave in later. Rep to make total of 9 scallops.

Turn and knit across all scallops: 90 (99, 108, 117) sts.

Knit 6 rows.

Beg patt and work even for 1".

Maintaining patt, inc 1 st at beg and end of every 8th row 3 times: 96 (105, 114, 123) sts. Work even in patt st until piece measures 9 (9, 10, 10)" from bottom of edging.

Beg sleeve shaping: Inc 1 st at beg of next 8 rows. CO 8 sts at beg of next 2 rows. CO 10 sts at beg of next 2 rows: 140 (149, 158, 167) sts.

Cont in patt until piece measures 18 (18, 20, 20)" from bottom of edging and armhole opening measures approx 7 (7, 8, 8)". End after a WS row.

Separate right and left shoulders: On next RS row, K62 (66, 71, 75) sts. BO center 16 (17, 16, 17) sts. Knit rem sts: 62 (66, 71, 75) on each shoulder.

Neck and shoulder shaping: At neck edge, BO 4 sts once, then BO 2 sts 3 times: 52 (56, 61, 65) sts. AT THE SAME TIME, on the shoulder edge, BO 10 (10, 11, 11) sts 3 times, then 11 (13, 14, 16) sts twice. Attach yarn at neck edge on other side. Rep neck and shoulder shaping.

KNIT WITH SUCCESS

The sheen of Pisa can make it slippery to handle, so to avoid tangles, Donna rolls it around a paper-towel core instead of winding it into a ball. Another time-saving technique she uses is to slip the yarn into a nylon knee-high stocking to keep it contained as she knits.

Bamboo or wooden needles provide more "stick" than do slick metal needles, making it easier to hold onto the ribbon and avoid dropped stitches. Slinky Pisa catches easily on rough surfaces, however, so keep an emery board and hand lotion in your ditty bag to prevent nails and rough skin from snagging the yarn as you knit.

Finishing

Sew shoulder and side seams.

Neckband: With RS facing and 16" circular needle, PU 80 sts. Work garter st in the round as foll: Knit odd-number rnds, purl even-number rnds. Work for 6 rnds. BO kw.

Armhole bands: With RS facing and 16" circular needle, PU 64 (64, 74, 74) sts. Work garter st in the round as for neckband. BO kw.

Weave in ends.

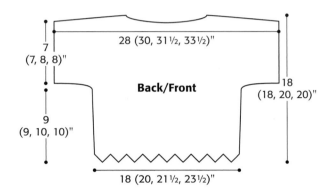

7 (7, 8, 8)"

28 (30, 31½, 33½)"

Back/Front

18 (18, 20, 20)"

9 (9, 10, 10)"

18 (20, 21½, 23½)"

OFF THE SHOULDER

By JoAnne Turcotte

Once during a National Needlework Association show, I had nothing new and luxurious to wear to the Galleria fashion show, so JoAnne whipped up this exotic tank for me—literally overnight. The rich, earthy shades of Java on the fringed ribbon inspired JoAnne to create a garment reminiscent of the back-to-nature setting of Tarzan and Jane. Wide flat, shiny fringed ribbon is perfect for this garment, creating a furry fabric with much shine and silkiness.

Stockinette stitch is all that is needed to produce a dazzling texture and color repeat with a wide, fringed ribbon. A complex stitch pattern would be lost in the texture. And while most yarns knit in stockinette stitch would curl at the bottom, the weight of the ribbon prevents that.

Except for the slanted bottom, the back and front of this unique top are identical. The slant adds a designer touch, but this project is still easy enough for a beginning ribbon knitter to achieve.

Knit with a fringed ribbon, this garment features a fun, furry look with loads of designer appeal. Garment is knit in colorway Java.

This version of Off the Shoulder is shown in Parrot ribbon from Plymouth Yarn Company.

Vital Statistics

Skill Level: Beginner

Finished Bust Measurement: 32 (36, 40, 44)"

Length: 19 (19, 20, 20)" measured along shortest side

Gauge: 2 sts = 1" in St st

Ribbon Type: Crossover (wide flat with fringe edges)

Materials

Yarn is from Cherry Tree Hill unless otherwise noted.

Yarn: 3 (4, 4, 5) hanks of Fringe (100% nylon; 4 oz; 62 yds) in colorway Java

or 8 (10, 12, 13) balls of Parrot (100% nylon; 50 g; 28 yds) in color 3 from Plymouth Yarn Company

Needles: US 15

Notions: Size I (5.5mm) crochet hook, stitch marker

Fringe (top) in colorway Java, and Parrot (bottom) in color 3

Front

Loosely CO 3 (5, 5, 6) sts.

Row 1 and all WS rows: Purl.

Note: Rows 2–16 involve CO additional sts as you knit. See "Cable Cast On" on page 102 for more information.

Row 2 (RS): CO 3 sts, knit entire row: 6 (8, 8, 9) sts.

Row 4: CO 3 (3, 4, 4) sts, knit entire row: 9 (11, 12, 13) sts.

Row 6: CO 3 (3, 4, 4) sts, knit entire row: 12 (14, 16, 17) sts.

Row 8: CO 3 (4, 4, 5) sts, knit entire row: 15 (18, 20, 22) sts.

Row 10: CO 4 (4, 5, 5) sts, knit entire row: 19 (22, 25, 27) sts.

Row 12: CO 4 (4, 5, 5) sts, knit entire row: 23 (26, 30, 32) sts.

Row 14: CO 4 (5, 5, 6) sts, knit entire row: 27 (31, 35, 38) sts.

Row 16: CO 5 (5, 5, 6) sts, knit entire row: 32 (36, 40, 44) sts.

Row 17: Purl. PM at side edge.

Cont in St st, work even for 4 rows.

Side shaping (RS): Dec 1 st at each side edge. Work 3 rows even. Rep last 4 rows once more: 28 (32, 36, 40) sts. Work 2 more rows even.

Inc 1 st at each side edge by knitting into front and back of first and next-to-last sts. Work 5 rows even. Rep inc row once more: 32 (36, 40, 44) sts.

Work even until total length from marker is 11½ (11½, 12½, 12½)", ending with WS row.

KNIT WITH SUCCESS

Fringe comes packaged in a hank, while Parrot, a similar ribbon, comes packaged in a ball. Neither ribbon is overly slippery. They're easy to contain because the fringed edges help them stay secure. Simply wind Fringe by hand and place it or prewound Parrot in a resealable plastic bag when not in use.

Fringe and Parrot are both easy ribbons to handle. Unlike some ribbons, they do not seem to have a mind of their own.

Armhole shaping: BO 2 sts at beg of next 2 rows: 28 (32, 36, 40) sts. Dec 1 st at each side edge on next row and every foll RS row 1 (2, 2, 2) more time: 24 (26, 30, 34) sts. End by working WS row.

Neck shaping (RS): Work across 9 (9, 10, 11) sts, BO next 6 (8, 10, 12) sts, work across rest of row. Work on 9 (9, 10, 11) sts of right shoulder only (this will be left shoulder when working sweater back) as foll:

***Row 1(WS):** Purl.

Row 2: Knit across row, dec 1 st at neck edge.

Row 3: Purl.

Rep last 2 rows 1 (1, 1, 2) more time: 7 (7, 8, 8) sts.

Work even in St st until total length is 19 (19, 20, 20)" from marker, ending with WS row. BO.**

Reattach yarn to left shoulder sts (right shoulder sts when working the back) at neck edge, ready to work WS row. Finish as for other shoulder working from * to **.

Back

Loosely CO 3 (5, 5, 6) sts.

Row 1 and all RS rows (RS): Knit.

Row 2 (WS): CO 3 sts, purl entire row: 6 (8, 8, 9) sts.

Row 4: CO 3 (3, 4, 4) sts, purl entire row: 9 (11, 12, 13) sts.

Row 6: CO 3 (3, 4, 4) sts, purl entire row: 12 (14, 16, 17) sts.

Row 8: CO 3 (4, 4, 5) sts, purl entire row: 15 (18, 20, 22) sts.

Row 10: CO 4 (4, 5, 5) sts, purl entire row: 19 (22, 25, 27) sts.

Row 12: CO 4 (4, 5, 5) sts, purl entire row: 23 (26, 30, 32) sts.

Row 14: CO 4 (5, 5, 6) sts, purl entire row: 27 (31, 35, 38) sts.

Row 16: CO 5 (5, 5, 6) sts, purl entire row: 32 (36, 40, 44) sts.

Row 17: Purl. Place marker at side edge.

Work remainder of back as for front.

Finishing

Sew shoulder and side seams.

Using crochet hook, sc around bottom edge (see "Crochet" on page 102).

Weave in all ends.

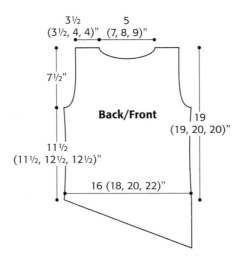

The front and back of this tank top are identical except for the direction of the angled bottom, which means you can wear either side as the front.

HAVE IT BOTH WAYS

By Terri Shea

This pair of T-shirt tops gives you the option to knit a garment from side to side or from back to front. In each design, the same two ribbons and two additional novelty yarns were combined for a rich texture; only the colorway is different. But notice how the direction of the knitting moves the colors differently through the garment. Each of the yarns and ribbons used in a garment is dyed in the same colorway, but because different fibers take the same dyes differently, the finished garments have a unique shaded look. The ribbon, especially the tubular Pisa ribbon, creates shimmer that moves through the fabric.

While the two tops use the same shapes and features, they drape differently due to the direction of the knitting. Terri used seed stitch to avoid any noticeable striping and to provide textural interest without requiring special edging. These luxurious tops can be worn alone or with a jacket or shawl for a more formal look.

The back-to-front knit tee (left) is shown in colorway Moody Blues, and the side-to-side knit tee (right) is shown in Spanish Moss. Both use the same pattern stitch and the same two ribbons combined with two novelty yarns, but in different colorways.

Seed stitch is a very forgiving and stretchy knitting pattern. You may want to choose a size that's close to your natural bust measurement so that your sweater won't droop undesirably.

SIDE-TO-SIDE OPTION

Vital Statistics

Skill Level: Intermediate

Finished Bust Measurement: 32 (36, 40, 44, 48)"

Length: 17¾ (19¾, 20¾, 21, 22)"

Gauge: 16 sts and 27 rows = 4" in seed st

Ribbon Types: Cashcott—crossover (wide flat, ladder); Pisa—tubular

Materials

Yarns are from Cherry Tree Hill.

Yarn:

A—1 (1, 2, 2) hanks of Melange (75% rayon/25% cotton; 8 oz; 272 yds) in colorway Spanish Moss

B—1 (1, 2, 2) hanks of Silk & Merino Worsted (50% silk/50% merino blend; 4 oz; 278 yds) in colorway Spanish Moss

C—2 (2, 2, 3) hanks of Cashcott (100% nylon; 4 oz; 140 yds) in colorway Spanish Moss

D—1 (1, 2, 2) hanks of Pisa (100% nylon; 4 oz; 248 yds) in colorway Spanish Moss

Needle: US 10 circular needle, 29" long, or size needed to obtain gauge

Notions: Size D (3.25mm) crochet hook, tapestry needle

From top to bottom: Melange, Silk & Merino Worsted, Cashcott, and Pisa are all in colorway Spanish Moss.

Seed Stitch (Multiple of 2)

Row 1 (RS): *K1, P1; rep from * to end.

Row 2: *P1, K1; rep from * to end.

Rep these 2 rows for patt.

Yarn Sequence

Work yarns in the foll order:

2 rows A (Melange)

2 rows B (Silk & Merino Worsted)

2 rows C (Cashcott)

2 rows D (Pisa)

Note: This large piece of knitting will seem shapeless and stretchy while you're working. However, when side seams are sewn and the neck and hem are finished with crochet, the fabric will hold in place.

Right Sleeve and Right Body

Using A, CO 52 (54, 54, 56, 56) sts. Work in seed st, changing yarns EOR per yarn sequence above. Don't cut yarn between rows, just carry it loosely up side of knitting; loops from carrying yarn can be sewn down when seaming.

Inc at beg and end of row every 4th row 10 times: 72 (74, 74, 76, 76) sts.

CO 45 (52, 56, 56, 60) sts at end of next 2 rows (you will need to cut yarns and reattach them during next yarn sequence): 164 (180, 188, 190, 198) sts on needle. Work even for 4½ (5½, 6½, 7½, 8½)", ending on a WS row.

Neck Shaping and Left Body

Work in patt for 62 (70, 74, 75, 79) sts for front then BO 24 sts and work rem 77 (85, 89, 90, 94) sts for back. Work back only in patt for 7", ending with a WS row.

Turn work so that WS is facing. Work front in est patt, attaching yarns in order, with ends at hemline, not neck edge. Work front for 7". (Count rows for accurate matching of front to back.) When front is same length as back, work across piece, CO 24 sts for neck/shoulder, and work back sts: 164 (180, 188, 190, 198) sts on needle. Work even for 4½ (5½, 6½, 7½, 8½)", ending on WS row.

Left Sleeve

BO 45 (52, 56, 56, 60) sts at beg of next 2 rows: 72 (74, 74, 76, 76) sts rem.

Dec at beg and end of every 4th row 10 times: 52 (54, 54, 56, 56) sts rem.

BO all sts in patt.

Finishing

Weave in ends.

Spritz with water, pin to measurements, cover with towel, and let sit overnight to dry.

Sew sleeve and side seams using yarn B.

With RS facing, use crochet hook and yarn C to work sc around hem and neck edges, covering yarn ends and loops formed by carrying yarns up side of work. Work 2nd round of sc, dec 3 sts at each corner of neck. Cut yarn and weave in end.

Note: Neck needs to be crocheted very firmly. Work as many additional crochet rounds as desired for smaller neck opening, and feel free to change yarns as desired.

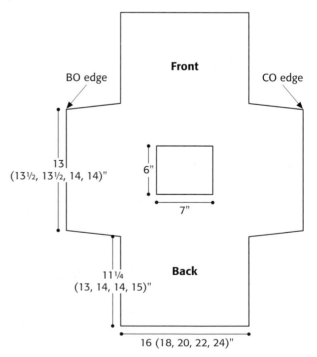

This large piece of knitting may seem shapeless and stretchy while you're working. Don't panic; when the side seams are sewn and the neck and edges finished with crochet, it will hold in place.

BACK-TO-FRONT OPTION

Vital Statistics

Skill Level: Intermediate

Finished Bust Measurement: 32 (36, 40, 44, 48)"

Length: 18¾ (19¾, 20¾, 20¾, 21¾)"

Gauge: 16 st and 27 rows = 4" in seed stitch

Ribbon Types: Cashcott—crossover (wide flat, ladder); Pisa—tubular

Materials

Yarns are from Cherry Tree Hill.

Yarn:

A—1 (1, 2, 2) hanks of Melange (75% rayon/25% cotton; 8 oz; 272 yds) in colorway Moody Blues

B—1 (1, 2, 2) hanks of Silk & Merino Worsted (50% silk/50% merino blend; 4 oz; 278 yds) in colorway Moody Blues

C—2 (2, 2, 3) hanks of Cashcott (100% nylon; 4 oz; 140 yds) in colorway Moody Blues

D—1 (1, 2, 2) hanks of Pisa (100% nylon; 4 oz; 248 yds) in colorway Moody Blues

Needle: US 10 circular needle, 29" long, or size needed to obtain gauge

Notions: Size D (3.25 mm) crochet hook

From top to bottom: Melange, Silk & Merino Worsted, Cashcott, and Pisa, all in colorway Moody Blues

Seed Stitch (Multiple of 2)

Row 1 (RS): *K1, P1; repeat from * to end.

Row 2: *P1, K1; repeat from * to end.

Repeat these 2 rows for patt.

Yarn Sequence

Work yarns in foll order:

2 rows A (Melange)

2 rows B (Silk & Merino Worsted)

2 rows C (Cashcott)

2 rows D (Pisa)

Back

With A, CO 64 (72, 80, 88, 96) sts. Work in seed st, changing yarns EOR according to yarn sequence above. Don't cut yarn between rows, just carry it loosely up side throughout garment, even during sleeve increases; loops will be hidden when seaming and crocheting edges.

Work in patt until piece measures 12 (13, 14, 14, 15)" or desired length to armhole, ending with WS row.

Inc for Sleeves

Continuing in seed st and changing yarn EOR, turn work so that RS is facing. CO 3 sts in old yarn color, using cable CO method (see page 102). Work row as est. Next row, with WS facing, CO 3 sts, then work row as est. Cont in this manner, CO 3 sts at beg of each row a total of 9 times: 27 sts added for each sleeve; 118 (126, 134, 142, 150) sts total on needle. Work even for 6½", ending with RS row.

Neck Shaping

Next WS row, work across 43 (47, 51, 55, 59) sts, BO center 32 sts, and complete row in patt. Work first shoulder only, in est patt, until sleeve edge measures 12", ending on WS row. Cut all yarns.

Next RS row, turn work so that WS is facing. Attaching yarns in order, work shoulder to match other side. (Count rows for accurate matching. The yarn-changing edge will be at sleeve cuff rather than neck edge.) When shoulder lengths match, work across first shoulder, CO 32 neck sts, then work across 2nd shoulder: 118 (126, 134, 142, 150) sts total. Work even for 1½".

Dec for Sleeves

BO 3 sts every row 18 times; 64 (72, 80, 88, 96) sts rem. Work even for 12 (13, 14, 14, 15)" or desired length to match back. BO all sts in patt.

Finishing

Finish as for Side-to-Side Option; see instructions on page 56.

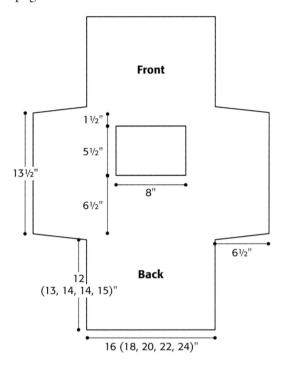

Front

1½"

5½"

13½"

8"

6½"

6½"

12 (13, 14, 14, 15)"

Back

16 (18, 20, 22, 24)"

KNIT WITH SUCCESS

To prepare the yarns for knitting, Terri wound the Pisa on a paper core made from two folded envelopes for good stability. Because she knit with four balls of yarn at once, she found it easiest to hand wind the other yarns into balls and secure them with a small hair clip when not in use. Each yarn knits at a slightly different gauge, so you'll need to adjust tension slightly. Using a blunt-tipped needle is advisable as the Melange tends to split when using a sharp needle.

Yarns not in use on each row are carried very loosely up the sides. Ribbon yarn is not as stretchy as others, so take extra care. With each yarn change, Terri worked three stitches and then adjusted the tension with her fingers so that the fabric edge could stretch without pulling. Don't worry about these loops of yarn—they will be hidden within the seam or single-crochet edging.

BAGS and KNAPSACKS

Ribbons aren't just for apparel. Knitted accessories give you a chance to work with ribbons in a whole new way, and many can be knit from ribbon scraps left over from larger projects. The variety of bags in this section provides a welcome change from the ubiquitous scarf, and what better yarn than ribbon for creating shimmering bags and pretty purses? Gauge and sizing are often not important—it's simply a matter of personal taste—which makes ribbon substitution simple and fun. Adorn these bags with beads and buttons, and you can create a unique and glamorous look in minutes.

STRING CARRYALL

By Donna Druchunas

When grocery shopping, Donna always asks for paper bags, which are more environmentally friendly than plastic, but she doesn't like how quickly they pile up in her garage. She recently learned that in Germany most people bring bags to the grocery store because plastic bags cost ten cents each. Suddenly she had a knitter's solution for her growing stack of brown paper.

What knitter wouldn't love an attractive ribbon-knit bag designed for quick trips to the store after work or to pick up a few extra ingredients for a favorite recipe? Economical and convenient, it folds up small enough to stash in a purse or briefcase, so you can always have it on hand when you shop.

Rainbow Ribbon is a durable, washable yarn that feels just as soft and comfortable as a favorite T-shirt. The yarn is easy to knit and requires no special handling. The tubular cotton mesh yarn is perfect for the openwork design of this trendy bag, resulting in a casual, fun accessory.

Carryall string bag is shown in Rainbow Ribbon in colorway Tropical Storm.

Vital Statistics

Skill Level: Intermediate

Size: Approx 9½" x 15", excluding straps

Gauge: Approx 12 sts = 4" in patt sequence

Ribbon Type: Tubular

Materials

Yarn is from Cherry Tree Hill.

Yarn: 2 hanks of Rainbow Ribbon (100% worsted-weight cotton; 4 oz; 262 yds) in colorway Tropical Storm

Needles: US 8 circular needle, 20" long, or size needed to obtain gauge; US 8 double-pointed needles

Notions: Stitch holder

Rainbow Ribbon in colorway Tropical Storm

Netting Stitch

Rnd 1: YO, *K2tog tbl, YO, rep from * around.

Rnd 2: K2tog, *YO, K2tog, rep from * around.

Rep rnds 1 and 2 for patt.

Drop-Stitch Garter Panel

Rnds 1, 2, 4, and 6: Knit.

Rnds 3 and 5: Purl.

Rnd 7: *K1 wrapping yarn 3 times; rep from * around.

Rnd 8: *K1 dropping YOs; rep from * around. Pull on bottom of knitting to elongate sts made from dropped YOs.

Rnds 9, 11, 13, and 14: Knit.

Rnds 10 and 12: Purl.

Rep rnds 1–14 for patt.

Bag Body

With circular needle, CO 80 sts. Join, being careful not to twist sts. *Work 14 rnds of netting st, then work 1 rep of drop-st garter panel; rep from* once.

Work 14 rnds of netting st.

Divide for front and back: K40, sl rem 40 sts to holder.

Front

Beg working back and forth in garter st (knit every row). AT THE SAME TIME dec 1 st at beg and end of every 4th row. Work until 24 sts rem. BO all sts.

Back

Sl sts from holder sts onto needle. Attach yarn and work as for front.

Side opening edging: With RS facing and using circular needle, PU 34 sts evenly spaced (17 sts on front and 17 sts on back) along opening on one side of bag. Knit 3 rows. BO all sts.

Rep side opening edging on other side of bag.

Handles

Beg I-cord: With dpn, CO 3 sts. *K3, do not turn, sl sts to other end of dpn, rep from * until I-cord measures 1".

Attach I-cord: K3, sl right needle into st on top edge of bag back. You now have 4 sts. *Slide sts to other end of dpn, K2, K2tog tbl (working 1 st from I-cord tog with 1 st from top of bag). Sl needle into next st at top edge of bag, rep from * until you can't pick up any more sts.

Work another 17" of unattached I-cord. BO and cut yarn.

CO 3 sts. Work attached I-cord as described above along top edge of entire strap. BO all sts.

Repeat to make I-cord handle for bag front.

Note: If you don't like to work attached I-cord, work entire length of strap in regular I-cord and sew pieces together.

Finishing

Sew ends of straps together, sew bottom seam, and weave in all ends.

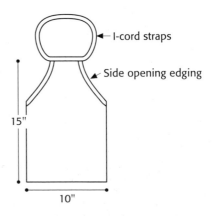

I-cord straps

Side opening edging

15"

10"

KNIT WITH SUCCESS

Although this yarn is easy to work with, bamboo needles are less slippery than metal ones, and they make the yarn-over rows easy to accomplish. After working a yarn-over row and the following row, pull on the bottom of the knitting to elongate the stitches made from the dropped yarn overs.

WINE BAG

By Donna Druchunas

Donna loves visiting wineries and admiring the beautiful picnic baskets, wine glasses, and gift bags available in their gift shops. When she saw the beautiful shimmer of Sachet ribbon, she was inspired to create this convivial bag. What better way to present a bottle of wine to your host or hostess at a holiday party or summer barbecue?

The shine and body of Sachet works well for this project for two reasons. The shimmer provides a beautiful and festive appearance, while the thickness of the ribbon offers durability and makes the wine bag a gift that the recipient will treasure for years to come.

This versatile gift bag makes a great housewarming gift and can be used again and again. Here, the wine bag is shown knit in Sachet in colorway Northern Lights.

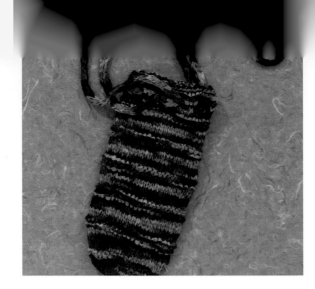

It takes just one hank of Sachet or Glitter Sachet to knit this wine bag, shown here in Glitter Sachet in colorway Dusk.

Vital Statistics

Skill Level: Beginner

Size: Approx 5" x 12"

Gauge: Approx 12 sts and 16 rnds = 4" in garter ridge patt

Ribbon Type: Wide flat

Materials

Yarn is from Cherry Tree Hill.

Yarn: 1 hank of Sachet (100% nylon; 4 oz; 121 yds) in colorway Northern Lights

or 1 hank of Glitter Sachet (99% nylon/1% metallic polyester; 4 oz; 131 yds) in colorway Dusk

Needles: US 11 double-pointed needles, or size needed to obtain gauge; US 11 circular needle, 16" long *(optional)*

Notions: Tapestry needle

Sachet (top) is shown in Northern Lights. Glitter Sachet (bottom) is shown in Dusk.

Garter Stitch (in the Round)

Rnd 1: Knit.

Rnd 2: Purl.

Rep rnds 1 and 2 for patt.

Garter Ridge Pattern

Rnds 1–6: Knit.

Rnd 7: Purl.

Rnd 8: Knit.

Rnd 9: Purl.

Rep rnds 1–9 for patt.

Bag

With dpn or 16" circular needle, CO 48 sts. Distribute sts evenly on 3 or 4 needles. Join, being careful not to twist sts.

Work 5 rnds of garter st in the round for top edge of bag, ending with knit rnd.

Work eyelets for straps: *K2, YO, K2tog, rep from * to end of rnd.

Work rnds 4–9 of garter ridge patt once.

Work rnds 1–9 of garter ridge patt 5 times.

If working on circular needle, change to dpn. Work dec to shape bottom of bag as foll:

Rnd 1: K6, K2tog, rep to end of rnd.

Rnd 2: K5, K2tog, rep to end of rnd.

Rnd 3: K4, K2tog, rep to end of rnd.

Rnd 4: K3, K2tog, rep to end of rnd.

Rnd 5: K2, K2tog, rep to end of rnd.

Rnd 6: K1, K2tog, rep to end of rnd.

Rnd 7: K2tog, rep to end of rnd.

Cut yarn, thread tail through rem sts, pull tight, and fasten off.

Straps (Make 2)

With dpn, CO 3 sts.

Work 3-st I-cord (see page 104) for 28" or desired length.

BO all sts.

Finishing

Weave straps in and out through eyelets. Sew ends of each strap tog to form a loop. Weave in ends.

Pull straps in opposite directions to close bag.

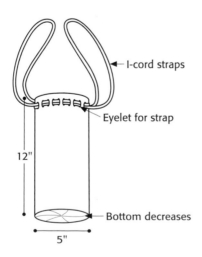

- I-cord straps
- Eyelet for strap
- 12"
- Bottom decreases
- 5"

KNIT WITH SUCCESS

Although Sachet and Glitter Sachet are easy to work with, knitters should be mindful of their open weaves. Both ribbons are wide with an airy texture, so take care to avoid piercing them with the point of your needle while knitting.

FRINGED CELL PHONE CASES

By Sharon Mooney

Sharon knew that any cell phone bag she created would have to be special due to the public's love affair with tiny wireless phones. She focused on a quilted pillow motif, perfect for adding beaded details. One hank of ribbon is enough to knit this design for both a small and a large phone, so you can choose the pattern that fits your particular phone, and then use the leftover yardage to make a carrier for a friend.

Unlike many ribbons, this cotton mesh with smooth matte finish offers the opportunity for great stitch definition, such as the quilted pillow stitch used for this little bag. Rainbow Ribbon also knits up into a bit denser fabric than other ribbons, which helps the bag maintain its shape. The all-cotton ribbon is durable and washable, and makes great twisted-cord straps and fringe.

A wearable-art cell phone case is fun to knit and even more fun to carry.

Large and small fringed bags are shown in Rainbow Ribbon in colorway Quarry Hill.

Vital Statistics

Skill Level: Intermediate

Size: Small (Large)

Width: Approx 3¼ (3¼)"

Length: Approx 4 (5¾)", excluding fringe and with front flap closed

Gauge: 20 sts and 32 rows = 4" in St st

Ribbon Type: Tubular

Materials

Yarn is from Cherry Tree Hill.

Yarn: 1 hank of Rainbow Ribbon (100% worsted-weight cotton; 4 oz; 262 yds) in colorway Quarry Hill for each bag

Needles: US 4 or size needed to obtain gauge

Notions: 43 (58) pony beads, size 6/0; sewing needle to fit through beads; sewing thread to match yarn; 1 button, 1" diameter; size E (3.5mm) crochet hook

Rainbow Ribbon in colorway Quarry Hill

Small Bag Instructions

CO 7 sts to begin front flap.

Row 1 (RS): Knit.

Rows 2–5: Inc 1 st at each end of row as foll: K1f&b, knit to last st, K1f&b: 15 sts at end of row 5.

Row 6 (buttonhole row): K1f&b, K6, YO, K2tog, K5, K1f&b: 17 sts.

Row 7: Rep row 2: 19 sts.

Rows 8–14: Knit.

Begin quilted patt (bag back) as foll:

Row 15 (RS): Knit.

Row 16: Purl.

Rows 17 and 18: Rep rows 15 and 16 once.

Row 19: K3, *(drop next st and unravel for 4 rows, insert left needle into dropped st and under 4 unraveled loops, knit this st tog with 4 loops, K3), rep from * to end.

Row 20: Purl.

Row 21: Knit.

Rows 22 and 23: Rep rows 20 and 21.

Row 24: Purl.

Row 25: K1, *(drop next st and unravel for 4 rows, insert left needle into dropped st and under 4 unraveled loops, knit this st tog with 4 loops, K3), rep from * to last 2 sts. Drop next st and unravel for 4 rows, insert left needle into dropped st and under the 4 unraveled loops, knit this st tog with 4 loops, K1.

Rows 26–30: Rep rows 20–24.

Row 31: Rep row 19.

Rows 32–37: Rep rows 20–25.

Rows 38–42: Rep rows 20–24.

Row 43: Rep row 19.

Rows 44–49: Rep rows 20–25.

Rows 50–54: Rep rows 20–24.

Row 55: Rep row 19.

Rows 56–60: Rep rows 20–24.

Row 61: This is eyelet row for bottom folded edge: K1, *(YO, K2tog), rep from * to end.

Rows 62–66: Rep rows 20–24.

Beg quilted patt (bag front) as foll:

Row 67: Knit.

Row 68: Purl.

Rows 69 and 70: Rep rows 67 and 68.

Row 71: Rep row 19.

Rows 72–77: Rep rows 20–25.

Row 78–82: Rep rows 20–24.

Row 83: Rep row 19.

Rows 84–89: Rep rows 20–25.

Rows 90–94: Rep rows 20–24.

Row 95: Rep row 19.

Rows 96–101: Rep rows 20–25.

Rows 102–105: Rep rows 20–23.

Row 106: Knit.

BO all sts.

Large Bag Instructions

CO 7 sts to begin front flap.

Row 1 (RS): Knit.

Rows 2–5: K1f&b, knit to last st, K1f&b: 15 sts at end of row 5.

Row 6 (buttonhole row): K1f&b, K6, YO, K2tog, K5, K1f&b: 17 sts.

Row 7: Rep row 2: 19 sts.

Rows 8–16: Knit.

Begin quilted patt (bag back) as foll:

Row 17 (RS): Knit.

Row 18: Purl.

Rows 19 and 20: Rep rows 15 and 16.

Row 21: K3, *(drop next st and unravel for 4 rows, insert left needle into dropped st and under 4 unraveled loops, knit this st tog with 4 loops, K3), rep from * to end.

Row 22: Purl.

Row 23: Knit.

Rows 24 and 25: Rep rows 22 and 23.

Row 26: Purl.

Row 27: K1, *(drop next st and unravel for 4 rows, insert left needle into dropped st and under 4 unraveled loops, knit this st tog with 4 loops, K3), rep from * to last 2 sts, drop next st and unravel for 4 rows, insert left needle into dropped st and under 4 unraveled loops, knit this st tog with 4 loops, K1.

Rows 28–32: Rep rows 22–26.

Row 33: Rep row 21.

Rows 34–38: Rep rows 22–26.

Row 39: Rep row 27.

Rows 40–63: Rep rows 28–39 twice.

Rows 64–68: Rep rows 22–26.

Row 69: Rep row 21.

Rows 70–74: Rep rows 22–26.

Row 75 (eyelet row/bottom fold line): K1, *(YO, K2tog), rep from * to end.

Row 76–80: Rep rows 22–26.

Begin quilted patt (bag front) as foll:

Row 81: Knit.

Row 82: Purl.

Rows 83 and 84: Rep rows 81 and 82.

Row 85: Rep row 21.

Rows 86–90: Rep rows 22–26.

Row 91: Rep row 27.

Row 92–96: Rep rows 22–26.

Row 97: Rep row 21.

Rows 98–121: Rep rows 86–97 twice more.

Row 122–126: Rep rows 22–26.

Row 127: Rep row 27.

Row 128: Purl.

Row 129: Knit.

Rows 130 and 131: Rep rows 128 and 129.

Row 132: Knit.

BO all sts.

KNIT WITH SUCCESS

Rainbow Ribbon is so easy to handle that with few exceptions it's like knitting with regular yarn. You can easily use an umbrella swift and ball winder to make quick work of winding this yarn. Knitting too tightly with cotton ribbon can cause it to bunch up, so Sharon recommends holding the strands loosely and paying attention to your tension. The ribbon twists naturally. If you find this bothersome, just hold the ball and let the knitting dangle to slowly unwind on its own.

Finishing (Both Sizes)

With RS tog, sew side seams using yarn and tapestry needle, leaving triangular flap free. Cut yarn end to 6" and weave through sts to secure. Weave in all loose yarn ends. Cut off excess yarn.

Fringe: Cut 20 lengths of yarn, 4" long. Arrange in sets of 2. To make each fringe, hold 2 lengths of yarn together and fold in half. Insert crochet hook through first eyelet opening at bottom fold of bag. Grab fold of yarn with hook and pull through eyelet opening. Grab loose ends of yarn with hook and pull through fold of yarns. Rep 9 more times across bottom fold of bag. Trim ends of fringe even.

Twisted-cord strap: Cut a 120 (240)" length of yarn. Fold in half and attach fold over a doorknob, or have someone hold the fold for you. Knot loose ends of yarn about ½" from ends. Twist knotted end until yarn starts to twist back on itself. Hold center of twisted length of yarn and fold in half again. This will cause yarn to twist around itself forming twisted cord. Cut off knot previously made. Knot each end 2" above ends of yarn. Leave ends of yarn for fringe, but trim them evenly. Sew strap end securely in place at top of each side of bag using sewing needle and thread. Secure cord above and below knot. The finished cord will be approximately 18 (44)" long (excluding fringe at each end).

Beads: Using sewing needle and thread, sew 1 bead in center of each quilted pillow on front and back of bag.

Button closure: Using sewing needle and thread, sew button securely on front of bag under buttonhole.

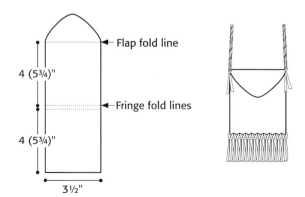

4 (5¾)" — Flap fold line

4 (5¾)" — Fringe fold lines

3½"

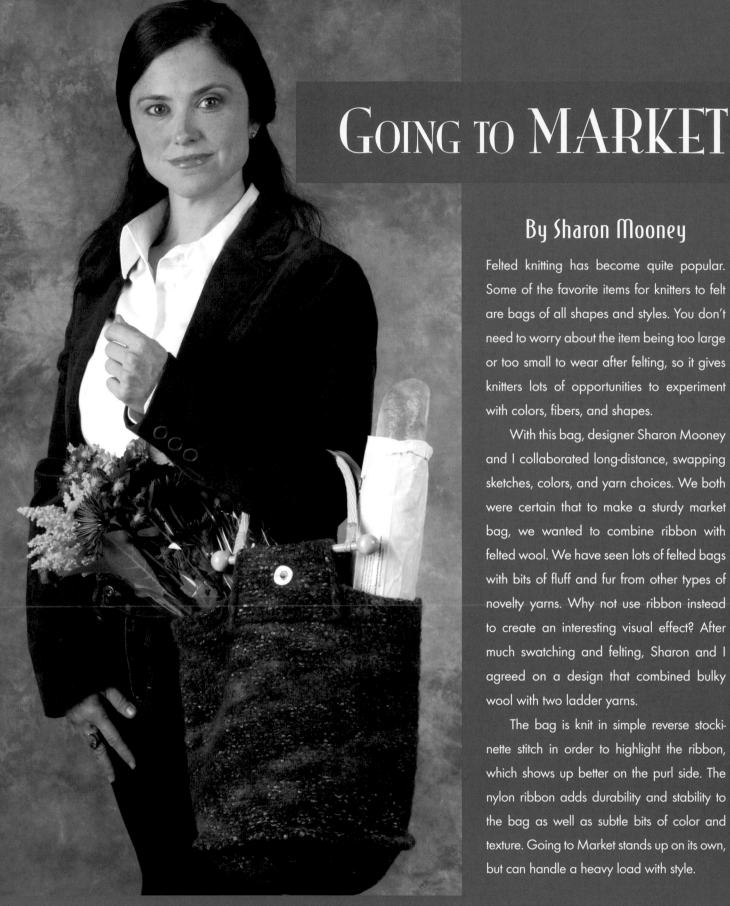

GOING TO MARKET

By Sharon Mooney

Felted knitting has become quite popular. Some of the favorite items for knitters to felt are bags of all shapes and styles. You don't need to worry about the item being too large or too small to wear after felting, so it gives knitters lots of opportunities to experiment with colors, fibers, and shapes.

With this bag, designer Sharon Mooney and I collaborated long-distance, swapping sketches, colors, and yarn choices. We both were certain that to make a sturdy market bag, we wanted to combine ribbon with felted wool. We have seen lots of felted bags with bits of fluff and fur from other types of novelty yarns. Why not use ribbon instead to create an interesting visual effect? After much swatching and felting, Sharon and I agreed on a design that combined bulky wool with two ladder yarns.

The bag is knit in simple reverse stockinette stitch in order to highlight the ribbon, which shows up better on the purl side. The nylon ribbon adds durability and stability to the bag as well as subtle bits of color and texture. Going to Market stands up on its own, but can handle a heavy load with style.

The Going to Market bag is shown in Windsong and Zebra Windsong in colorway Gypsy Rose and Potluck Bulky in color family Jewels.

Combining fancy ribbon with basic bulky wool dresses up
this durable and functional bag.

Vital Statistics

Skill Level: Intermediate

Size after Knitting: Approx 16¾" (just above
flange) x 15¾" (from top edge to bottom of
flange)

Size after Felting: Approx 14" (just above
flange) x 13" (from top edge to bottom of flange)

Gauge: 12 sts and 19 rows = 4" in St st

Ribbon Type: Ladder

Materials

Yarn is from Cherry Tree Hill.

Yarn:

A—2 hanks of Windsong (100% nylon; 50 g; 165
yds) in colorway Gypsy Rose

B—1 hank of Zebra Windsong (100% nylon; 50
g; 165 yds) in colorway Gypsy Rose

C—3 hanks of Potluck Bulky (100% wool; 4 oz;
200 yds) in potluck color family Jewels

Needles: US 11 double-pointed needles; US 11
circular needle, 24" long; US 6 circular needle,
24" long, for picking up flange stitches

Notions: Split-ring stitch marker; stitch holder
or spare needle; tapestry needle; hand-sewing

needle and thread; set of rattan purse handles
(shown are JoAnn Sew Essentials Rattan Handles
with 5" area for felted handle cover); 2 buttons,
⅞" diameter

Windsong (top) and Zebra Windsong (center), both in
colorway Gypsy Rose; Potluck Bulky (bottom)
in color family Jewels

Bag Instructions

Always hold together 1 strand each of the 2 yarns
indicated throughout. When changing yarns, leave
a 6" tail for weaving in.

Handle Covers (Make 2)

With size 11 circular needle and one strand each of
A and C, CO 20 sts.

Row 1: Purl.

Row 2: Knit.

Rows 3–26: Rep rows 1 and 2 twelve times.

Row 27: Purl.

Place sts on holder while you knit 2nd handle
cover. Cut yarns, leaving 6" length of each for
weaving in.

Body of Bag

Row 28: With size 11 circular needle and B and C, CO 12 sts, K20 from 1 handle cover, CO 25 sts, K20 from rem handle cover, CO 13 sts: 90 sts total. PM and join to knit in rnds.

Work in garter st in the round for 8 rnds. (Knit odd rnds, purl even rnds.)

Rnd 9: (K18, M1) rep around: 95 sts.

Rnd 10: Purl.

Rnds 11–19: With C and A, purl.

Rnd 20: P10, *(M1, P9) rep from * around: 100 sts.

Rnd 21: Purl.

Rnds 22–32: With C and B, purl.

Rnds 33–43: With C and A, purl.

Rnds 44–58: With C and B, purl.

Rnds 59–75: With C and A, purl.

Use C and A to end of bag.

Flange

With size 6 circular needle, PU 1 st 5 rows directly below first st on WS of left-hand size 11 needle you've been knitting with. Cont to PU sts 5 rows directly down from sts on WS of size 11 needle all the way around to marker.

Rnd 76: (Place right-hand size 11 needle through first st on left-hand size 11 needle and then through first st on size 6 needle, and purl these 2 sts tog) rep to end of rnd.

Bottom of Bag

Rnd 77 and all odd-numbered rnds: Purl.

Rnd 78: (P18, P2tog) rep around: 95 sts.

Rnd 80: (P17, P2tog) rep around: 90 sts.

Rnd 82: (P16, P2tog) rep around: 85 sts.

Rnd 84: (P15, P2tog) rep around: 80 sts.

Rnd 86: (P14, P2tog) rep around: 75 sts.

Rnd 88: (P13, P2tog) rep around: 70 sts.

Rnd 90: (P12, P2tog) rep around: 65 sts.

Rnd 92: (P11, P2tog) rep around: 60 sts.

Rnd 94: (P10, P2tog) rep around: 55 sts.

Rnd 96: (P9, P2tog) rep around: 50 sts.

Rnd 98: (P8, P2tog) rep around: 45 sts.

Rnd 100: (P7, P2tog) rep around: 40 sts.

Rnd 102: (P6, P2tog) rep around: 35 sts.

Rnd 104: (P5, P2tog) rep around: 30 sts.

Rnd 106: (P4, P2tog) rep around: 25 sts.

Rnd 108: (P3, P2tog) rep around: 20 sts.

Rnd 110: (P2tog) rep around: 10 sts.

KNIT WITH SUCCESS

Both Windsong and Zebra Windsong behave better during knitting if you wind them around a paper towel core before use. Take care not to split the ribbon with the tip of your needle when knitting it together with the Potluck wool. Keep the tension loose as you knit. If you knit too tightly, you will be fighting with your knitting during the entire project. And don't worry about the ribbon twisting as you knit, because only glimpses of it will show through the felted fabric.

finishing

Cut yarn and thread the ends through tapestry needle. Insert threaded needle through sts left on knitting needle in same order that you would have knit them. Pull tight to close bottom of bag and push the tapestry needle through to WS of bag. Weave through sts to secure. Weave in all loose yarn ends. Cut off excess yarn.

Felt bag: Set washing machine to hot water and small load setting. Add a couple of drops of wool wash (this will lubricate fibers). When washer starts to agitate, toss in bag with RS out. Let it agitate for about 5 minutes (no longer). Use tongs to remove bag from washer to check size. If you need to make bag smaller, throw it back in for another 3 to 5 minutes. Repeat this process until bag is size you want. (Squeeze out suds to get a good look.) When you achieve desired size, remove bag and gently squeeze out as much water as possible. Lay bag on thick towel. Roll towel around bag and lean on it to remove as much additional water as possible. Shape bag into barrel shape and stuff with bubble wrap or plastic grocery bags so that it keeps its form and stays upright while drying. You can continue to shape it as it dries, if necessary. It may take a day or two to dry completely.

Attach handles: Fold each handle cover over a handle. The handle cover will overlap RS of bag by about 1½". Using sewing needle and thread and backstitch for strength, sew each handle cover in place beginning just below encased handle ½" from edge of handle cover. End back stitching just below other side of handle. Bury knot ends in felt. Sew a button securely at center of each handle cover.

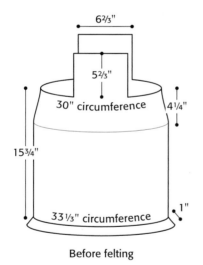

Before felting

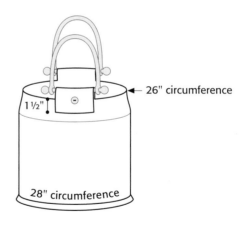

After felting

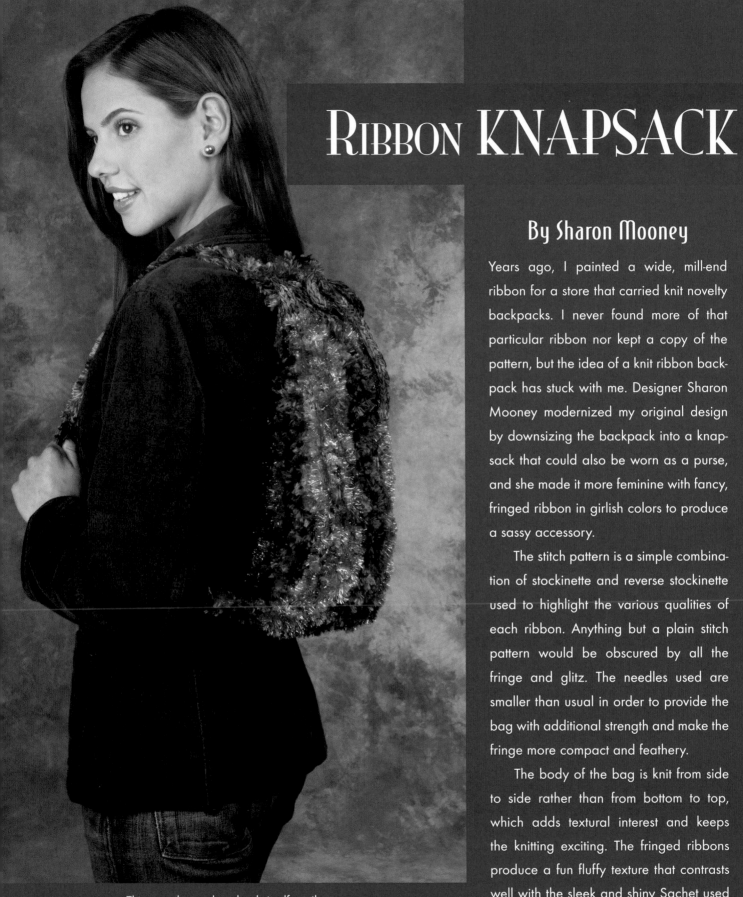

RIBBON KNAPSACK

By Sharon Mooney

Years ago, I painted a wide, mill-end ribbon for a store that carried knit novelty backpacks. I never found more of that particular ribbon nor kept a copy of the pattern, but the idea of a knit ribbon backpack has stuck with me. Designer Sharon Mooney modernized my original design by downsizing the backpack into a knapsack that could also be worn as a purse, and she made it more feminine with fancy, fringed ribbon in girlish colors to produce a sassy accessory.

The stitch pattern is a simple combination of stockinette and reverse stockinette used to highlight the various qualities of each ribbon. Anything but a plain stitch pattern would be obscured by all the fringe and glitz. The needles used are smaller than usual in order to provide the bag with additional strength and make the fringe more compact and feathery.

The body of the bag is knit from side to side rather than from bottom to top, which adds textural interest and keeps the knitting exciting. The fringed ribbons produce a fun fluffy texture that contrasts well with the sleek and shiny Sachet used to work the top of the bag in the round.

This over-the-top bag lends itself easily to alternate ribbon choices and substitutions.

The Ribbon Knapsack is knit from Fringe, Glitter Fringe, and Sachet, all in the same colorway. The varying shine and textures that differentiate the three ribbons are natural choices to emphasize in the design of this bag.

Vital Statistics

Skill Level: Intermediate

Size: Approx 10" x 14", excluding straps

Gauge: 12 sts and 16 rows = 4" in St st using Sachet and size 13 needles

Ribbon Types: Wide flat and wide flat with fringe

Materials

Yarns are from Cherry Tree Hill.

Yarn:

A—1 hank of Fringe (100% nylon; 4 oz; 62 yds) in colorway Winterberry

B—1 hank of Glitter Fringe (100% nylon; 4 oz; 62 yds) in colorway Winterberry

C—1 hank of Sachet (100% nylon; 4 oz; 121 yds) in colorway Winterberry

Needles: US 13 straight needles; US 13 circular needle, 16" long, or size needed to obtain gauge; US 11 double-pointed needles

Notions: Stitch marker; sewing needle and heavy-duty thread in color to match ribbon

Fringe (top), Glitter Fringe (center), and Sachet (bottom), all in colorway Winterberry

Body of Knapsack

When changing yarns, leave a 6" tail for weaving in.

With A, CO 25 sts.

Row 1 (RS): Knit.

Row 2: Purl.

Row 3: Knit.

Rows 4 and 5: Change to B and purl.

Row 6: Knit.

Rows 7 and 8: Rep rows 5 and 6.

Row 9: Purl.

Row 10: Change to A and purl.

Row 11: Knit.

Rows 12–15: Rep rows 10 and 11 twice. Cut A.

Rows 16–51: Rep rows 4–15 three times.

Rows 52–57: Rep rows 4–9 once.

Row 58: With A, purl.

Row 59: Knit.

Row 60: Purl.

BO all sts.

Sew BO edge to CO edge using yarn C. This seam will be at center back of knapsack. Sew bottom seam.

Top of Knapsack

Using circular needle and C, and with RS facing, PU 40 sts around top of knapsack body, beg at center back seam. PM and join to knit in rnds.

Rnds 1–7: (K2, P2) rep around.

Rnd 8 (eyelet rnd): (K2tog, YO, P2) rep around.

Rnds 9–12: Knit.

Rnd 13: Change to A, and knit.

BO all sts.

I-Cord Straps

With dpn and A, CO 3 sts. Work 3-st I-cord (see page 104) for 32". Make 2 for straps.

With dpn and C, CO 3 sts. Work 3-st I-cord for 32". Make 1 for drawstring.

Finishing

Cut yarn ends to 6". Weave end through sts to secure. Weave in all loose yarn ends. Cut off excess yarn. Using sewing needle and thread, sew one end of one strap to upper-right side of top of knapsack, just below eyelet row. Repeat with other strap on upper-left side of knapsack top. Sew other end of each strap to lower-right and lower-left corners of body, respectively.

KNIT WITH SUCCESS

All three of the wide ribbons used for this project knit at about the same gauge and are fun to combine. Because the knapsack can be knit proportionally in many different sizes, it is easy to substitute other ribbons for this project. To avoid tight stitches and bunching, be sure to carry yarns loosely when they're not in use.

The ribbons will begin to twist as you knit. If this becomes problematic, push the knitting away from the needle point and stand up, hold onto the knitting, and let the ball of yarn gently untwist without touching the floor.

Starting at center front of bag, weave drawstring through eyelet holes at top of knapsack so that ends both come out at center front of knapsack. Make ends even, pull tight, and tie into bow to close.

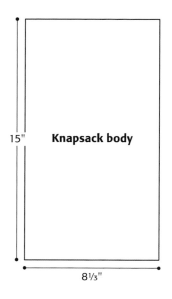

15"   **Knapsack body**

8⅓"

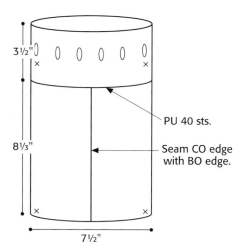

3½"   ○ ○ ○ ○ ○

PU 40 sts.

8⅓"

Seam CO edge
with BO edge.

7½"

Attach straps at back of bag at "×."

PONCHOS

Ponchos have overtaken the knitwear scene much as scarves did a few years ago. And like scarves, most are no longer knit for warmth and weather protection. They've been transformed into fashion accessories to complement any outfit, and many are designed without animal-fiber yarns. Like scarves, they are both trendy and timeless.

Ponchos are easy to knit because they usually require little in the way of shaping, and fit is not a critical issue. Sizing is more a matter of personal taste than of adhering strictly to body measurements. With the excellent drape and luster that ribbons provide, what better yarn than a luxury ribbon to show off a simple poncho shape?

EASY ONE-PIECE PONCHO

By JoAnne Turcotte

Ponchos are versatile garments that can be worn in various ways for any occasion. What JoAnne sought in this design was an avenue to emphasize the silkiness and shine of elegant wide ribbons. To do this, she chose a simple pattern stitch featuring dropped wraps that allow the yarn to show off in an open lacy fashion. Long, flowing strands of fringe add to the sleek, draped appearance.

A poncho needs to drape, and ribbon does it naturally. Wide flat ribbon gives this poncho a pleasing hand that could not be achieved easily with another fiber.

Shiny wide ribbons, such as the Sachet ribbon used here, lend drape to the simple style of this timeless poncho shown in colorway Blueberry Hill.

You can knit the same poncho design in machine-printed ribbon,
shown here in Jungle from Plymouth Yarn Company.

Vital Statistics

Skill Level: Intermediate

Finished Size: Approx 27" wide x 25" long
(after folding and seaming)

Gauge: 10 sts = 4" in garter st patt

Ribbon Type: Wide flat

Materials

Yarn is from Cherry Tree Hill unless otherwise noted.

Yarn: 4 hanks of Sachet (100% nylon; 4 oz; 121
yds) in colorway Blueberry Hill

or 8 balls of Jungle from Plymouth Yarn
Company (100% nylon; 50 g; 61 yds) in color
3257

Needles: US 15 or size needed to obtain gauge

Notions: Size J (6 mm) crochet hook

Sachet (top) in colorway Blueberry Hill,
and Jungle (bottom) in color 3257

Poncho Instructions

Loosely CO 63 sts, leaving 8" tail.

Rows 1–4: Knit.

Row 5: *(K1, YO), rep from * to last st, K1.

Row 6: Knit across, dropping all YOs.

Rep rows 1–6 for patt.

Work in patt until piece measures 54" or desired
length, ending with row 4.

Loosely BO all sts kw.

Finishing

Fold poncho in half with RS together and short
ends matching. Referring to diagram on page 84,
sew seam along top edge about 15" from open side
edges, leaving rem edge unsewn for neck opening.
Turn RS out.

Cut 46 pieces of ribbon, 20" long. Attach single
strands of fringe evenly spaced at 23 points along
the CO and BO ends of poncho (see "Fringe" on
page 104).

Weave in all ends.

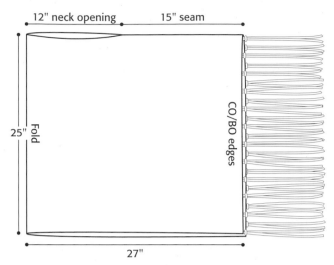

12" neck opening   15" seam

25"   Fold   CO/BO edges

27"

KNIT WITH SUCCESS

Jungle comes on a hard-core ball, and Sachet comes in hank form. Either can be used for this poncho, and both are slippery. Jungle is held in place by a rubber band, but once opened, it can be placed in a resealable plastic bag. Sachet can be hand wound into a ball, but it is advisable to place the hank around a swift or chair back before cutting the ties. Keeping the ball locked in a bag will prevent runaway ribbon.

Although they are easy to knit, keep your eye on these wide flat ribbons in order to keep them from dropping off the needles. Knitting a little more slowly than usual will help you keep the slippery ribbon in check. Any dropped stitches should be tended to quickly before they run down the knitting. Keep safety pins handy for locking up errant stitches.

Eros PONCHO AND RUFFLED SCARF

By Mavis Pakier

This beautiful poncho and scarf set is perfect for showcasing the narrow ladder-style yarns such as Eros and Zebra Windsong. What these two ribbons have in common is multiple colors over a black, tracked open weave, which provides elegant drape and sophisticated style. Both the poncho and matching scarf complement all figure types and can be dressed up with evening wear or dressed down with jeans.

Although the finished garments look rich and complex, they are easy to knit and moderate in cost. The poncho is knit in plain stockinette stitch, while a simple rib stitch gives body and dimension to the ruffled scarf. Eros and Zebra Windsong are interchangeable; no matter which yarn you choose, you'll enjoy the light weight and silky feel of the surprisingly solid knitted fabric that the open-weave yarn produces. Together or alone, these knit pieces make an elegant year-round fashion statement.

The Eros Poncho and Ruffled Scarf is shown in multicolored ladder ribbon, which knits into a very drapable fabric that suits all figure types.

The same poncho is shown in hand-painted Zebra Windsong in colorway Peacock from Cherry Tree Hill.

Vital Statistics

Skill Level: Intermediate

Finished Scarf Measurements: Approx 3" x 50"

Finished Poncho Measurements: Approx 20 (22, 24)" x 20 (22, 24)"

Finished Poncho Circumference: Approx 56 (62, 68)"

Finished Poncho Length: Approx 28 (31, 34)", excluding fringe

Gauge: 20 sts and 36 rows = 4" in St st on size 8 needles

Ribbon Type: Ladder

Materials

Yarn is from Cherry Tree Hill unless otherwise noted.

Yarn for Poncho: 5 (6, 7) balls of Eros from Plymouth Yarn Company (100% nylon; 50 g; 165 yds) in color 4796

or 5 (6, 7) hanks of Zebra Windsong (100% nylon; 50 g; 165 yds) in colorway Peacock

Yarn for Scarf: 2 balls of matching Eros *or* 2 hanks of matching Zebra Windsong

Needles: US 8 for poncho, or size needed to obtain gauge; US 8 and 10 for scarf

Notions: Size G (4 mm) crochet hook

Eros (top) in color 4796 and Zebra Windsong (bottom) in colorway Peacock

Poncho Front and Back
(make 2)

With size 8 needles, loosely CO 100 (110, 120) sts.

Row 1 (WS): Purl.

Row 2 (RS): Knit.

Rep these 2 rows until piece measures approx 12 (14, 16)", ending with WS row.

Neck shaping: Loosely BO 40 sts (this forms one side of V-neck and should measure approx 8"), and knit to end of row.

Cont in St st as est on rem 60 (70, 80) sts for another 8" from BO row, ending with WS row. This forms other side of V-neck. Total length from CO edge should be approx 20 (22, 24)".

Loosely BO rem 60 (70, 80) sts.

Ruffled Scarf is knit from Zebra Windsong in colorway Peacock.
Regular Windsong can be substituted too.

Finishing

Sew front and back tog along 12 (14, 16)" shoulder/side edges. The 8" edges will form V-neck opening.

Weave in all ends.

Neck edging: With RS facing, starting at top of left shoulder seam and using 2 strands of ribbon, sc along all 4 sides of V neckline (back and front). There should be approx 24 sc along each of 4 sides. Rep sc row 1 or 2 more times if desired to bring neckline higher. Next, work row of rev sc to form cordlike edge. Finally, work row of sl st crochet along V neckline in holes that were formed when last row of rev sc was worked. This will stabilize neckline and add decorative finished edge as well. Fasten off yarn and weave in all ends carefully and securely.

Fringe: Cut ribbon into 15" lengths. Attach 2 strands at a time to make fringe evenly spaced approx ½" apart around all sides of poncho (see "Fringe" on page 104).

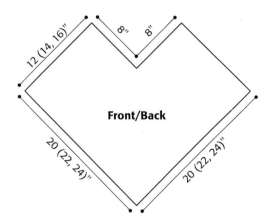

Ruffled Scarf

With size 10 needles, CO 99 sts.

Row 1 (WS): Purl.

Row 2: Knit.

Rep rows 1 and 2 for a total of 19 rows, ending with WS row.

Dec row: K3tog across row: 33 sts.

Change to size 8 needles and work in ribbing patt as foll:

Row 1 (WS): *(K1, P1), rep from * to last st, K1.

Row 2: K2, *(P1, K1), rep from * to last 3 sts, P1, K2.

Rep rows 1 and 2 until scarf measures 46" from CO, ending with WS row.

Inc row: (K1, P1, K1) in each st across row: 99 sts.

Next row: Purl.

Change to size 10 needles and cont in St st until ruffle is same length as beg ruffle (18 more rows), ending with WS row.

Loosely BO all sts. Weave in all ends.

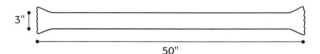

KNIT WITH SUCCESS

As with other slippery ribbons, keep these ladder ribbons in a resealable bag while knitting. To prevent your stitches from slipping off the needles, Mavis recommends that you use high-quality wooden needles and take care not to accidentally poke the tip of the needle through the open tracks of the yarn.

As with many ribbons, a little twisting is fine. If it becomes bothersome, take the yarn from the bag, put a rubber band around the ball, and hold up the knitting to let the weight of the ball slowly untwist the yarn.

While both pieces are easy to knit, accurate measuring is crucial because the poncho is designed to be a perfect square. It pays to become adept at counting ribbon rows and to bind off loosely so that the poncho hangs evenly.

CROSSOVER PONCHO

By Carla Esden-Tempska

Carla fell in love with the texture and drape of the Cashcott and Windsong combination she used for the Crossover Shawl and decided that the same two ribbons would be perfect for a lightweight poncho. Like many knitters, she loves knitting but not sewing the pieces together, so she devised a poncho knit in one piece. The three-needle bind-off technique is used to finish the only seam.

Like her shawl, Carla's poncho employs seed stitch and alternating rows of the two ribbons to blend the textures, creating a durable fabric that drapes nicely. Carla wears hers constantly. Since she lives in Florida where it sometimes gets too hot to wear even a lightweight outer garment, she appreciates that this poncho can be taken off and tossed into a handbag. It holds up well, looking as great as ever when she retrieves it to take the chill off an air-conditioned room.

Flattering and easy to wear, this versatile poncho is suitable for year-round wear almost anywhere.

The Crossover Poncho is shown knit in Cashcott and
Windsong, both in colorway Fall Foliage.

Vital Statistics

Skill Level: Easy

To Fit Bust: S/M (M/L): 32–36 (38–42)"

Gauge: 7 sts = 4" in patt st

Ribbon Types: Cashcott—crossover (wide flat,
ladder); Windsong (narrow ladder)

Materials

Yarns are from Cherry Tree Hill.

Yarn:

A—2 (3) hanks of Cashcott (100% nylon; 4 oz;
140 yds) in colorway Fall Foliage

B—1 (2) hank of Windsong (100% nylon; 50 g;
165 yds) in colorway Fall Foliage

Needles: US 15 or size needed to obtain gauge

Notions: Size J (6 mm) crochet hook; stitch
holder; spare needle

Cashcott (top) and Windsong (bottom),
both in colorway Fall Foliage

Stitch Patterns

Seed Stitch

Row 1: *K1, P1, rep from * to end.

Row 2: *P1, K1, rep from * to end.

Twisted Drop Stitch

Put right-hand needle through next st on left needle
as if to knit. Wrap yarn around both needles once.
Then wrap yarn around right-hand needle only
and complete stitch by pulling the right-needle
wrap through both loops on left needle.

Poncho Instructions

Using A, CO 70 (78) sts.

Beg patt row sequence as foll:

> **Rows 1 and 2:** Using 2 strands of B, work 2
> rows seed st.
>
> **Rows 3 and 4:** Using 1 strand of A, work 2
> rows seed st.
>
> **Rows 5–8:** Rep rows 1–4.
>
> **Rows 9 and 10:** Rep rows 3 and 4.
>
> **Rows 11 and 12:** Knit.
>
> **Row 13:** Work 1 row twisted drop st.

Row 14: Knit.

Rows 15–18: Rep rows 1–4.

Rows 19–24: Repeat rows 9–14.

Cont in seed st patt sequence (rep rows 1–4) until piece measures 12 (14)", ending with row 1.

Cont with A, work 25 (29) sts in seed st and place sts on holder.

Loosely BO next 20 (20) sts.

Work the rem 25 (29) sts in seed st.

Change to 2 strands of B and cont seed st patt beg with row 3 for another 5": 17 (19)" total.

Work rows 9–14.

Work rows 1–4.

Work rows 9–14.

Resume seed st patt (rows 1–4) and work until piece measures 24 (28)", ending with row 2.

Sl sts from holder onto a needle so that first worked st will be on outside edge of garment.

KNIT WITH SUCCESS

In this garment, the Windsong yarn is knit with two strands held together. When doubling the Windsong, it is helpful to put both balls of yarn in a resealable plastic bag. Keep the Cashcott in a separate bag.

Finishing

Fold knitted piece so that 2 needles are next to each other and fabric is not twisted. Each needle should have 25 (29) sts, with outside edges closest to point of needles. You can finish with 3-needle BO (see page 105), or do the foll: Using a 3rd needle, purl 2 edges tog by moving 1 st from front needle to back needle and purling it tog with first st on back needle. Finish st as you normally would, moving new st onto right needle. Rep until all sts are used, purling loosely so that seam will not pucker. BO all sts loosely.

Fringe: Cut rem A into 20"-long pieces for fringe. Using 2 pieces of A for each fringe, attach strands of fringe approx 1" apart along the entire outer edge (see "Fringe" on page 104).

Optional: Work 1 row of dc around neck to strengthen it.

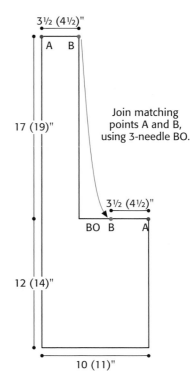

3½ (4½)"

A B

17 (19)"

Join matching points A and B, using 3-needle BO.

3½ (4½)"

BO B A

12 (14)"

10 (11)"

TWO-BY-TWO CONVERTIBLE

By JoAnne Turcotte and Cheryl Potter

When my friend and knitwear designer Barbara Venishnick passed away unexpectedly, JoAnne and I decided to collaborate on a poncho to replace Barbara's unfinished design for this book. Fortunately, I had Barbara's original sketch and swatch, and saw that she had envisioned a Mexican serape, which is an ample shawl that can wrap different ways to resemble a poncho.

We liked how designer Carla Esden-Tempska created the Crossover Poncho based on her pattern for the Crossover Shawl. We took her idea a step further and knit a one-piece shawl that you can transform into a poncho simply by lacing the side edges together with ribbon.

To add textural interest to the garment, we chose two yarns that normally aren't combined: a narrow nylon ribbon called Baby Sachet and a much wider regular Sachet. Because these yarns have widely different gauges, two needle sizes were required to obtain the rectangular shape. Sachet was worked with size 17 needles and Baby Sachet with size 10 needles. If you have never knit this way before, we urge you to try it!

This versatile shawl does double duty as a poncho when you lace the edges. Wear the laced seam at the shoulder or in the center front or back for a number of different looks.

Thin ribbon Baby Sachet and thicker Sachet require
different needle sizes in the same pattern.

Vital Statistics

Skill Level: Intermediate

Size: Approx 20" x 55"; one size fits all

Gauge: 14 sts = 4" in patt st and combination of
yarns and needles

Ribbon Types: Wide flat and narrow flat

Materials

Yarns are from Cherry Tree Hill.

Yarn:

A—2 hanks of Baby Sachet (100% nylon; 4 oz;
346 yds) in colorway Foxy Lady

B—3 hanks of Sachet (100% nylon; 4 oz; 121
yds) in colorway Foxy Lady

Needles: US 10 and 17 or size needed to obtain
gauge; US 10½ for CO and BO

Notions: Size J (6 mm) crochet hook

Baby Sachet and Sachet, both in colorway Foxy Lady

Poncho/Shawl Instructions

Cut 80 strands of Baby Sachet, 20" long, and set
aside for fringe. Cut 5 strands of Sachet, 20" long,
and set aside for ties.

Using size 10½ needles and A, CO 200 sts.

Rows 1–4: Change to size 10 needles, knit with A.

Rows 5 and 6: Change to size 17 needles and B,
K1, *(YO, K2tog); rep from * to last st, K1.

Rep rows 1–6, changing needles and yarns as indicated. Carry unused yarn loosely up side edge.

Work until B is used up and total length is approx
20" to 22". Work 4 more rows of A.

Change to size 10½ needles and BO with A. The
CO edge and BO edge should have same elasticity
to produce same width.

Finishing

Weave in all ends.

With five 20" strands of A in group, attach 8
groups of fringe evenly spaced along each short
end (see "Fringe" on page 104).

Tie the long edges together about every 4" to 5"
with five 20" strands of B. The draping of the
fabric will cause dips or holes to appear along the
top edge, a lovely style feature. Alternately, you
can untie the garment to wear as a shawl.

Optional finishing: If you prefer to turn garment permanently into a poncho, you can stitch the shoulder seam rather than lace it. Fold knitted piece in half with short ends aligned and sew seam along top edge. Start seaming at fringed edge and sew for about 15", leaving rem edge unsewn for neck opening. Weave in ends.

KNIT WITH SUCCESS

Stitches can seem very loose on the rows where you change from one size ribbon to another. As the gauge changes because of ribbon size, gently pull on the fabric to "lock" the ribbon into place. You may find it slow going on the rows where you need to knit from the smaller needles onto the much larger ones. To facilitate these changeover rows, try grabbing the stitch with the tip of your needle from the base of the stitch, where it is the most open.

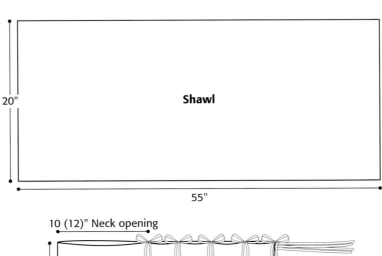

20"

Shawl

55"

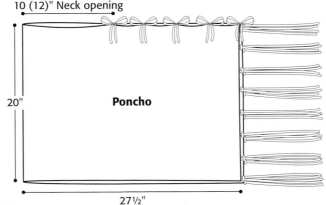

10 (12)" Neck opening

20"

Poncho

27½"

EXTREME PONCHO AND HAT

By Joyce Clark

Joyce wanted to create a simple but dynamic garment, so she chose a high-contrast color scheme and heavily textured ribbons. On the practical side, her goal was to design a poncho that draped nicely without hugging the body, with the ability to stay in place. To accomplish that, she combined three different wide nylon ribbons for the body of the poncho and added a silk merino for fringe. The fringed ribbons lend a fun, furry effect to the garment, and each yarn adds a different intensity to this funky poncho, allowing you to make a colorful statement.

The poncho is knit in a combination of stockinette and garter stitches designed to show off each yarn. The loose fit is over-sized for outerwear, but is not heavy or bulky. The coordinating hat completes this over-the-top ensemble.

The hat was knit using the gauge swatch for the poncho. The garments are knit in Silk & Merino Bulky, Fringe, Glitter Fringe, and Cashcott, all in colorway African Grey.

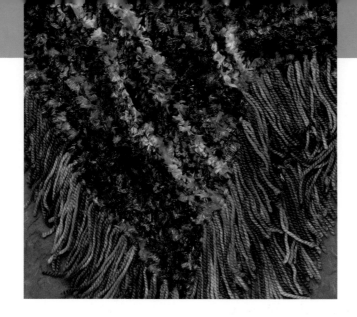

Extreme Poncho

Vital Statistics

Skill Level: Intermediate

To Fit Bust: One size fits most

Size: Each rectangle is approx 14" x 32½"

Gauge: 8 sts = 4" in garter st patt

Ribbon Types: Glitter Fringe and Fringe (both are wide flat with fringe); Cashcott—crossover (wide flat, ladder)

Materials

Yarns are from Cherry Tree Hill in colorway African Grey.

Yarn:

A—2 hanks Glitter Fringe (99% nylon/1% metallic polyester; 4 oz; 62 yds)

B—2 hanks Fringe (100% nylon; 4 oz; 62 yds)

C—1 hank Cashcott (100% nylon; 4 oz; 143 yds)

D—1 hank Silk & Merino Bulky (50% silk/50% merino; 4 oz; 140 yds)

Needles: US 13 or size needed to obtain gauge

Notions: Size I (5.5 mm) crochet hook

Top to bottom: Glitter Fringe, Fringe, Cashcott, and Silk & Merino Bulky, all in colorway African Grey. Each yarn has a different texture and tension.

Eyelet Lace Pattern

*P2tog, YO, rep from * across row, ending with P1.

Poncho Rectangles (make 2)

With A, CO 65 sts and knit 2 rows.

Change to C, work 4 rows in eyelet lace patt.

Change to A, knit 2 rows.

Change to C, work 4 rows in eyelet lace patt.

Change to B, knit 4 rows.

Change to C, work 4 rows in eyelet lace patt.

Change to B, knit 4 rows.

Change to C, work 4 rows in eyelet lace patt.

Change to A, knit 4 rows.

Change to C, work 4 rows in eyelet lace patt.

Change to B, knit 6 rows.

Total rows worked: 42. Loosely BO kw with B.

Finishing

Referring to diagram, sew 2 rectangles together. Weave in all ends. Cut yarn D into 10"-long pieces. Attach 2 strands tog for each fringe approx ½" apart along entire bottom edge (see "Fringe" on page 104).

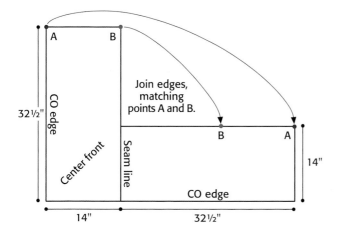

KNIT WITH SUCCESS

The most challenging aspect of knitting the Extreme Poncho is keeping the various yarns from twisting within themselves and tangling with each another. When working with several balls of ribbon at once, Joyce separates them like naughty children. She places them in individual plastic sandwich bags or knee-high stockings. She then puts one on each side of her and another in her lap in order to knit across a row while controlling twists and snarls. She likes the way ribbon twists as she works because the texture and color spectrum of the ribbons change as they twist. However, to avoid too much twisting, Joyce turns her knitting in the same direction at the end of each row throughout the entire project.

Joyce also recommends keeping a nail file handy when knitting with ribbons because they can easily snag on fingernails.

EXTREME HAT

The Extreme Hat is knit with leftover yarn from the poncho. You can customize it with an antique button if desired.

Vital Statistics

Skill Level: Intermediate

Size: One size fits most

Ribbon Types: Combination—Glitter Fringe and Fringe (both are wide flat with fringe); Cashcott (wide flat, ladder)

Gauge: 8 sts = 4" in garter st

Materials

Yarn: Use rem A, B, and D yarns from poncho

Needles: US 13 or size needed to obtain gauge

Notions: Tapestry needle

Hat Instructions

Alternate garter st and St st throughout as indicated.

With A, CO 40 sts and work 10 rows in garter st.

Change to D, work 4 rows in St st.

Change to B, work 10 rows in garter st.

Change to D, work 4 rows in St st.

Change to A, work 10 rows in garter st.

Change to D, work 4 rows in St st.

Change to B, work 6 rows in garter st.

Dec row: K2tog across row: 20 sts rem.

Thread a tapestry needle and pull yarn through all 20 sts.

Finishing

Sew back seam, reversing seam on last 10 rows of garter st.

Turn up brim and tack in place.

Special TECHNIQUES

In this section you'll find a compilation of special techniques used in *Ribbon Style*. The descriptions are by no means exhaustive, but you may find them handy for quick reference. Use the short glossary that follows to familiarize yourself with new terms or check abbreviations for stitches and techniques you may already know.

Cable Cast On (cable CO)

To cast on stitches to a work that's already in progress, such as to add sleeve stitches to a one-piece T-shirt, the cable cast-on method is a quick and easy option.

At the beginning of a row of knitting, insert the right needle between the first two stitches on the left needle, wrap the yarn around the needle as if to knit, and pull the new loop through to the front and place it on the end of the left needle to form one new stitch. Repeat for the number of stitches required.

Insert needle between 2 stitches.
Wrap yarn as if to knit and
pull loop through to front.

Place new stitch
on left needle.

Crochet

Crochet is often used in conjunction with knitting for finishing edges, making embellishments, adding buttonholes, and joining seams.

Chain Stitch

To begin, make a slipknot. Place the yarn over the hook and draw through the loop on the hook to start the chain. Repeat for desired number of chain stitches.

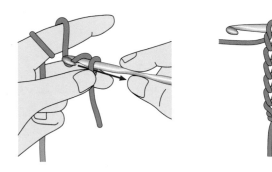

Single Crochet (sc)

Single crochet is often used to join seams. A crocheted seam tends to lie flat and adds little bulk.

To single crochet, begin with a chain stitch. Insert the hook into the previous knit or crochet stitch. Place the yarn over the hook and draw it through the stitch. You now have two loops on the hook. Place the yarn over the hook and draw the yarn through both loops on the hook. A single crochet stitch is complete.

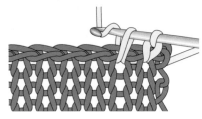

Insert hook into stitch, yarn over hook,
pull loop through to front, yarn over hook.
Pull loop through both loops on hook.

Reverse Single Crochet (rev sc)

Reverse single crochet gives the stitches a twisted appearance. The edge will be slightly raised, making a nice decorative finish for bound-off or cast-on edges.

To work reverse single crochet, with right side facing, insert the crochet hook into the first knitting below the cast-on or bound-off edge, starting at the left end of your work. Wrap yarn over the hook, pull the loop through the knitting, wrap yarn over the hook again, and pull through both loops on the hook. One stitch is made. Repeat, working from left to right to the end of the row or round.

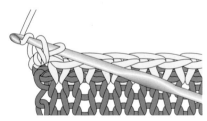

Join yarn with slip stitch.
Insert hook into first stitch
to the right.

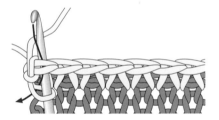

Yarn over hook, pull through
both loops on hook.

Double Crochet (dc)

Double crochet can also be used as an edging, although the edge will look more like a bound-off edge or a chain stitch than the more finished-looking reverse single crochet stitch.

To work double crochet, wrap the yarn around the crochet hook and then insert the crochet hook into the edge of the knitting as for single crochet, wrap the yarn over the hook, and pull the loop through the work. Wrap the yarn over the hook again and pull it through two of the loops on hook. Wrap the yarn over the hook again and pull it through remaining two loops to complete the stitch. Repeat across the edge or around the neckline.

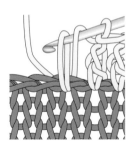

Yarn over hook, insert hook
into stitch, yarn over hook,
pull through to front.

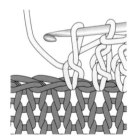

Yarn over hook, pull
through 2 loops on hook.

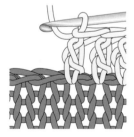

Yarn over hook, pull through
remaining 2 loops on hook.

Slip Stitch Crochet (sl st crochet)

To stabilize a neck edge or shoulder seam, work a row or round of slip stitch crochet as follows. Working from right to left, insert the crochet hook into the first stitch of knitting, wrap the yarn over the hook, and pull the loop of yarn through the stitch. *Insert the hook into the next stitch of knitting, wrap the yarn over the hook, pull the loop of yarn through the knit stitch and also through the loop of yarn on the hook.* Repeat from * to * for the length of the seam or around the neckline.

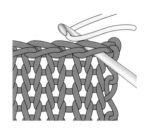

Insert hook into stitch,
yarn over hook.

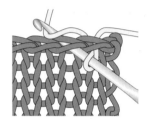

Insert hook into stitch,
yarn over hook.

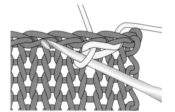

Pull loop of yarn through stitch
and loop on hook.

Fringe

To attach the fringe, fold the two strands in half, insert the crochet hook from the back to the front of the shawl, and pull folded end through the knitted fabric. Then hook the tail ends of the fringe, and pull them through the loop formed at the folded end of the fringe. Pull tight to secure.

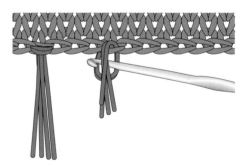

I-Cord

Knitted cord is often called I-cord, and it is made using double-pointed needles, although a circular needle can also be used. This cording is handy for making decorative items such as the purse straps or ties shown on page 76.

1. Cast on two, three, or four stitches, per the project instructions.

2. Knit all stitches, but do not turn the work. Slide the stitches to the other end of the needle.

3. Repeat step 2 until the cord is the desired length; bind off all stitches.

Increases

Increases (and decreases) are used to shape various parts of a knitted project, such as armholes or necklines on a sweater. The following types of increases are used in this book.

Make 1 (M1)

Insert the right needle under the bar of yarn between the last stitch knit and the next stitch to be knit. Lift the bar onto the left needle and knit into the back of the stitch. One stitch has been made.

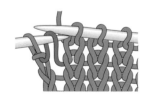

Insert left needle from front to
back through "running thread."

Knit into back of stitch.

Knit in Front and Back of Stitch (K1f&b)

Insert the right needle into the designated stitch on the left needle where the increase is to be made. Knit as usual, but do not slip the original stitch off of the left needle. Move the right needle behind the left needle and knit into the back of the same stitch. Slip the original stitch off the left needle; two new stitches have been made on the right needle.

Knit into stitch but do not drop it off left needle.

Knit into back of same stitch.

Three-Needle Bind Off (3-needle BO)

The three-needle bind off is used to join shoulder seams in one step, rather than binding off both the front and back stitches and then sewing them together. The result is a less bulky seam.

Place knitted pieces right sides together with needles parallel and pointing in the same direction. Knit one stitch from the front needle and one stitch from the back needle together. Repeat, and then pass the first stitch knit over the second stitch to bind off one stitch. Continue in the same manner until all stitches have been bound off.

 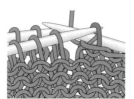

Knit together 1 stitch from front needle and 1 stitch from back needle.

Bind off.

ABBREVIATIONS

approx	approximately
beg	begin(ning)
BO	bind off or bound off
CO	cast on
cont	continue
dc	double crochet
dec	decrease(ing)
dpn(s)	double-pointed needle(s)
EOR	every other row
est	established
foll	follow(s)(ing)
g	gram(s)
garter st	garter stitch
inc	increase(ing)
K	knit
K1f&b	knit in front and back of stitch—an increase
K2tog	knit 2 stitches together—a decrease
K3tog	knit 3 stitches together—a decrease
kw	knitwise
m	meter(s)
M1	make 1 stitch: knit a stitch on horizontal bar between last stitch worked and next stitch on left needle—an increase
mm	millimeter(s)
oz	ounce(s)
P	purl

patt	pattern
p2sso	pass 2 slip stitches over next knitted stitch on right needle
P2tog	purl 2 stitches together—a decrease
PM	place marker
PU	pick up and knit
pw	purlwise
rem	remain(ing)
rep(s)	repeat(s)
rev sc	reverse single crochet
rev St st	reverse stockinette stitch
rnd(s)	round(s)
RS	right side
sc	single crochet
sl	slip
sl st	slip stitch (crochet)
SM	slip marker
ssk	slip 1, slip 1, knit these 2 stitches together—a decrease (slip both sts as if to knit)
st(s)	stitch(es)
St st	stockinette stitch
tbl	through back loop
tog	together
WS	wrong side
yd(s)	yard(s)
YO	yarn over

Skill Levels and Conversions

Skill Levels

Beginner: Projects for first-time knitters using basic knit and purl stitches. Minimal shaping.

Easy: Projects using basic stitches, repetitive stitch patterns, simple color changes, and simple shaping and finishing.

Intermediate: Projects with a variety of stitches, such as basic cables and lace; simple intarsia; double-pointed needles and knitting-in-the-round techniques; and midlevel shaping and finishing.

Metric Conversion

Use these handy formulas to easily convert yards to meters, or vice versa, so you can calculate how much yarn you'll need for your project.

Yards x .91 = meters

Meters x 1.09 = yards

Grams x 0.0352 = ounces

Ounces x 28.35 = grams

About the Project DESIGNERS

Joyce Clark

owns the Knit 'n' Hook yarn shop in Huntington, West Virginia. She began knitting during her early childhood and applies the serenity it offers throughout her daily life. She has taken many classes and workshops to perfect her knitting skills, and she now teaches others at her shop where many of her original-design garments are displayed.

Donna Druchunas

lives near the foothills of the Colorado Rocky Mountains, where she spends most of her time writing and knitting. Her designs and articles have been featured in most of the major knitting publications, and she is the author of *Arctic Lace* and *The Knitted Rug*. Visit her Web site at www.sheeptoshawl.com.

Carla Esden-Tempska

is a knitwear and jewelry designer who first learned to knit while in college. She rediscovered knitting when she fell in love with hand-painted yarns and opened the Chez Casuelle design studio in 2003. When she introduced her original designs on the Internet, she received so many requests from knitters that Chez Casuelle quickly turned into an online store for hand-painted yarns and kits. She lives in Lady Lake, Florida, and at www.chezcas.com.

Sharon Mooney

prefers knitting to any other activity. At the age of seven, she knit her first project, a rug for Barbie. She has designed both cross-stitch and knitting patterns, and now owns a pattern company called Knitting Knoodle. In her spare time, she works at the Enchanted Unicorn yarn shop in Redlands, California. You can visit her on the Web at www.knittingknoodle.com.

Mavis Pakier

is a California designer who does freelance design work and runs workshops for several of the top Southern California yarn shops. Mavis also loves to travel, and she develops many of her design ideas during visits to exotic places.

Jill Ramos

has been knitting since she was eight years old and has designed patterns for various yarn companies over the years. A former computer consultant, Jill now works at Saratoga Needle Arts in Saratoga Springs, New York, where she teaches knitting classes. In her spare time, she is also an ice skating instructor.

 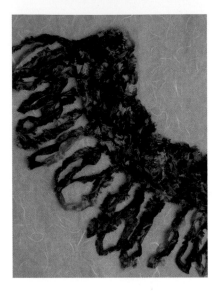

Terri Shea

designs knitwear from her home in Seattle, Washington. She loves knitting for women and children, and she designs classic-styled patterns that are logical and easy to work.

JoAnne Turcotte

is Design Director for Plymouth Yarn Company. She has been knitting for over 40 years and designing patterns for more than half of that time. JoAnne was trained and educated as a chemist, and she worked in materials engineering before finding her niche in the knitting world. In her spare time, JoAnne still teaches knitting classes at a Pennsylvania yarn shop near her home.